Kitchen Garden Living

Quarto.com

© 2025 Quarto Publishing Group USA Inc.
Text © 2025 Bailey Van Tassel

First Published in 2025 by Cool Springs Press, an imprint of The Quarto Group,
100 Cummings Center, Suite 265-D, Beverly, MA 01915, USA.
T (978) 282-9590 F (978) 283-2742

Cool Springs Press titles are also available at discount for retail, wholesale, promotional, and bulk purchase. For details, contact the Special Sales Manager by email at specialsales@quarto.com or by mail at The Quarto Group, Attn: Special Sales Manager, 100 Cummings Center, Suite 265-D, Beverly, MA 01915, USA.

29 28 27 26 25   1 2 3 4 5

ISBN: 978-0-7603-8899-0

Digital edition published in 2025
eISBN: 978-0-7603-8900-3

Library of Congress Cataloging-in-Publication Data is available.

Design: Allison Meierding
Cover Image: Kami Arant Photography
Page Layout: Megan Jones Design
Photography: Kami Arant Photography except by Caitlin Kraina on pages 158 and 161 and Dave Jakovich on page 30
Illustration: Abigail Diamond

Printed in China

Kitchen Garden Living

**SEASONAL GROWING AND EATING FROM
A BEAUTIFUL, BOUNTIFUL FOOD GARDEN**

BAILEY VAN TASSEL Founder of The Kitchen Garden Society

COOL
SPRINGS
PRESS

DEDICATION:

For Boyd, Georgia, and Duke.

You inspired me to begin, and you
continue to lead me daily in the practice
of pure love, presence, and authenticity.

Contents

◄ The summer garden in full swing with climbing Trombincino squash climbing our metal arch.

Introduction

It's an age-old tale. I grew up on a little hobby farm, and once I was old enough to leave, I vowed never to return. I even used to tell prospective clients in my post-graduate sales job about my upbringing and quickly learned that everyone loved the country-to-city schtick. I would recall how, with me, the apple fell far from the tree. My parents' little hobby farm in the northern part of California had working mules and horses in the pasture for team roping and wagon-pulling, chickens and pigs for feeding the family—the whole nine yards. But I wanted to move to the city, hear the click of my high heels on a busy sidewalk, and carry a chic leather briefcase. I was not charmed by the bucolic days of my childhood and longed for life in the fast lane. Everyone in those sales meetings would chuckle at the classic coming-of-age tale when I shared it, but little did I know how much I would change a few short years later and how hard I would try to get back to the very place I once so desperately longed to run away from.

Leaving my small town was the big dream . . . until it wasn't. It was the first of many hollow accomplishments that led me right back to where I started. It was within the first few years of living the fast life that I became disillusioned with the glitz, seeing it for what it was—a papier-mâché facade with little to back the color-coordinated suits and well-painted faces. I landed for a time in Hollywood, and while the big letters in the hillside still take my breath away, the allure of that lifestyle chipped away as quickly as a manicure in spring.

It took more than ten years after leaving our little farm town for the apple in me to reveal that

it had, in fact, fallen just below the canopy. I started to long for the simple, sweet life I was born into, one where there were actual apple orchards. The nearby orchard I grew up visiting belonged to dear neighbors of ours who brought me home from school on days when my parents worked late. We'd run through the fruit trees around their house and come in for hot grilled cheese and tomato soup. Friends were like family and we all belonged to each other. When the phrase "salt of the earth" was coined, it was in honor of those people—my people—the farmers and hard-working families of Sebastopol, California.

Me at three years old in my parents' garden in Sebastopol, California.

There's some magic in the place I called home as a child. I'm not the only one to know this, as Sonoma County is home to some of the world's best pinot noir, the redwood forests, the Russian River, and the Pacific Ocean. You can hike in the fog, eat oysters, walk vineyards, get fresh goat cheese, see the opera in San Francisco for the night, or get lost and go foraging up in the forest of Occidental. We will all tell you: We were the last generation to have a true childhood. We ran through blackberry tunnels, got rough redwood bark burns from falling down tree trunks, and ran in packs at the volunteer fire department fundraisers where a band would sing Credence Clearwater Revival while smoke from the Santa Maria barbecue flavored our corn and giant turkey legs. Something about that place wove itself into the fiber of my soul, like a glittering thread, ready to be pulled when the time was right.

That time did eventually come, just after I got married, when my husband and I were starting to really talk about having children and how and where we would raise them.

Having landed somewhat permanently along the sandy shores of Southern California, I found myself disenchanted with my surroundings. I realized, as many of us do, that my parents were right about everything. That the slow life, the *intentional life*, was indeed what "it" was all about. I felt trapped by the culture I was in, watching The Real Housewives of my own Orange County showcase exactly who I didn't want to become. At the time I was working with the mega-wealthy and was coordinating luxury international excursions, fundraising for philanthropic causes, and hosting live events for hundreds of entrepreneurs and CEOs. I even led an evening with the president of Rwanda as a guest speaker.

What I witnessed first-hand was this overwhelming access to money but an absolute underwhelm of connectedness to nature, to living in harmony with the seasons, and to having an awareness around soil, food, and resources. I yearned to deeply breathe in fresh air when

The front door of our first home opened up to the two raised beds that we built on our community's shared land.

everyone around me seemed to be running an entirely different race. It made me homesick for the people and the place that raised me, and it sent me on a quest to uproot everything and go find a farm to cultivate. What I really knew was that I could oh-so-easily succumb to this culture, too. I could fall into step keeping up with the Joneses, trading "old" designer purses in for new models each season and lose sight of what once felt so cleanly principled to me. Because of how close I was to the edge, I wanted to bake something into my life that demanded I keep my priorities intact. I wanted something to hold me accountable to my roots and my values, leaving little room for excess and drama.

One day my husband and I were talking about real estate. We had been debating this for months and I was really starting to push forward with this farm idea. We had just welcomed our first child into the world, and I felt deeply like I needed to raise him in the wild. I explained how I needed 3 acres (12,100 m^2) with a creek running through it for our baby to get lost on. I needed a huge garden like my Aunty Pammy had and maybe just two mini donkeys and some chickens. We learned quickly in those early days of marriage and children how much we each longed to recreate the parts of our childhood that we loved.

Humoring me, my husband, Joe, told me, "Bailey, even if you had the space for a huge garden, how do you know you'd even like gardening? How do you know this wouldn't just be a phase?" I'd never actually grown anything, and he wasn't wrong to challenge me on that. I'm known to be a bit of an enthusiastic hobbyist, quickly casting aside my current fixation for a fun new craft or project. I was certainly dreaming about something I hadn't ever shown interest in before and hadn't lived in for about a decade. I was so removed from that lifestyle, but yet I knew. I knew I was meant to return to my roots in some way, so hands on my hips and furrow in my brow, I marched straight to the closest place I knew to get plants and bought a one-pot garden. It was about 18 × 18 inches (46 × 46 cm) and had one tomato plant, one pepper plant, one basil plant, chives, and parsley.

I was in love and obsessively doted on this tiny, one-pot "garden," if you could even call it that. I watched as the leaves dropped from too little water, eventually harvesting one single tiny pepper and two tomatoes. I don't remember what happened to the rest of the plants, but I eventually got a bigger pot for the tomato. After that, I was able to convince our homeowners association to let us build two raised beds in front of our townhouse on a patch of dead communal lawn. We not only had to pay for the entire endeavor, but I also promised to use our own water, since the perpetual drought in California only allowed each family a certain amount of water usage. For a year, I dragged a 100-foot (30.5 m) expandable hose from the back of the house, through our living room, and out the front door to water my beds. We were throwing distance from a freeway and flanked by in-patient rehab centers, but once that garden was built, I felt like we had recreated the Garden of Eden with endless possibilities. It was like I built a room onto the house where I could live inoculated from the trappings of the actual place. It changed everything for me.

My son Boyd and I watering our first garden in the front of our townhouse.

Just like that, the glittering thread was pulled loose, and it began to weave a new tapestry whose image was clear. I started living again by the ways of the land, using the shifts in weather as a guide for the cadence of our life. I had my son beside me, my own little apple, not even a year old and learning the soil with me, taking trips to the plant nursery, and eating straight out of the garden. Together we amended that soil, picked cabbage loopers off broccoli, and discovered how even in the forever summer of Southern California, leaves fell. In the winter periods of my own life, ripe with loss, failure, uncertainty, and change, the garden taught me how to keep growing, how to welcome new children and teach them how to notice the scent of oncoming rain and the difference between ripe and not ready. Lessons I myself had when I was tiny.

I discovered my own way of living in tune with nature even amongst the concrete and crowded freeways. The kitchen garden had inspired a way of life that felt familiar and nostalgic yet completely brand new. A cadence developed where I would start the day with watering and interrupt the preparation of each meal to run outside and

The garden can be your sanctuary, even in the thick of having and raising children.

snag herbs or onions or a few cherry tomatoes. I felt like an anchor had been thrown in, tethering me to the sun, the rain, the lettuce, and the soil. Each day was a new opportunity to see how beautiful it is to grow in season and in an appropriate time. A new sense of awe was revealed that showed wild practicality. Planting a seed, watching it sprout, tending to it, and then finally harvesting and eating it—a completely ordinary occurrence. The simple purpose of the plant being the plant is nothing special, but getting to place this into my life and giving it meaning in our meals opened me up to the ordinary magic that we all need daily to survive the mundane.

You and I begin together now, like I once did, to rediscover how to embrace days marked by the rhythm of the seasons, at the mercy of nature, and in cocreation with age-old patterns. No matter where you live, or how big your garden is, there is a place for you to come alive. Character is not born out of convenience, but out of a dedication to something of inner value and a pursuit of truth.

Kitchen garden living is about placing the garden as a cornerstone in our lives, a place from which we draw inspiration, connect to and learn

A NOTE FOR THOSE IN THE THICK OF IT

Do this. Start your garden and start it now. There is no better time. This is not a task for the retired or a gift for the final chapter of your life. Gardening, especially kitchen gardening, is indelibly tied to our journey back to the dining table. It is the soul's work. It is the antidote to the frenzied and frazzled, to the empty vaults of a "full" calendar bankrupt of quality time. We are so plagued by the trappings of futures that may never come to be that we forget about the today that's right in front of us. Promises of escaping into the digital world, however imaginary, are growing increasingly "real" in their ability to rob us of knowing the feel of our feet on the ground and our hands in the dirt. My learning years in the garden were accompanied by children, all under the age of six, pulling me back inside for snacks, bringing home colds and fevers, taking us to and from activities and school drop offs and pick-ups—not to mention my own work. Now is the time to bask in the wonder of the growing world, to return yourself to a place where you're enchanted and caring for something that is entirely ungraspable.

For many, you only get one season in which you can grow food. If you start today, how many summers will you have to learn how to cultivate a cucumber—thirty, perhaps? Or twenty? Most things in life that we love and that love us back get many more than twenty or thirty opportunities to be practiced. The garden gives one shot a year to lean into its offerings. So, among the caregiving and the sleepless nights, return to the garden that gifts you and those around you with skills and a magic that endures and transcends the generations beside you and beyond you.

from the land, celebrate traditions new and old, and create a home around the bounty and brilliance of our backyard (or front yard, like I once did). It's about taking a centuries-old priority and practice and inserting it into our busy lives for the sake of, and perhaps in spite of, ourselves.

Together, in these pages, we'll start a garden from scratch and explore how to bring it to life, letting it inspire our days. There's gardening, and then there's *kitchen* gardening, which involves all sorts of usefulness and joy for ourselves and others in a way that is uniquely satisfying. We'll learn to start seeds, place plants, tend to the garden, and harvest, each in unique ways specific to the variations you'll encounter wherever and whatever you grow. We'll begin to see our days through the lens of what's in season, and what's growing in tandem with the flow of our own lives. We'll create a sense of place and return to work done by our own hands. We'll lean into the seasons.

This book is meant to be a companion for gardeners of all levels, helping you fold gardening into everyday life. With projects, tried and true tips, and easy concepts, I hope to solidify your know-how and instill a love of growing food and flowers by planting an ever-present "seed" that you can go on to share again and again, like those of an apple.

XO,
Bailey

CHAPTER 1

SEASONS

The seasons earmark our days like the chapter headings in a book. They give us a place to pause and dogear life, folding into a new rhythm guided by the elements. Because our lives are always changing within those evermoving seasons, home can be a steady force that provides us with comfort and a sense of place.

Being from the southern part of California, we don't have typical seasons. When the rest of the country is pulling out their cable-knit sweaters and grabbing their fluffy down comforters out of the attic, we're settling in for two more months of heat. Thanksgiving dinner is enjoyed outside, away from the hot oven that's been roasting our turkeys all day.

Because of our lack of typical seasons, it's extra important for our family to find ways to celebrate the passage of the traditional seasons and spot the changes in our landscape, small as they are. Allowing our bodies and minds to either rest or ramp up is vital in maintaining a healthy flow of life. Our souls get weary when we're always on the go in a place where there is no stopping for storms at midday or for a frost that quells the garden's growth. Instead, we must insert rest as the calendar dictates.

On the flip side, there is also a place for the quickening of life and making sure that our productivity is for a purpose, taking us toward our goals and into the traditions and celebrations that we crave and enjoy.

I recall a dear friend of mine explaining her children's Waldorf education to me in a beautiful way that I'll never forget. It informed how I now view our own day-to-day. She told me about how the children's days are built around the concept of inhales and exhales. Inhales are a calming, steadying gentleness. They bring us to center, calling for restoration. Exhales are the release, filled with movement, activity, exploration, and doing. In many ways, this is how we interact with the seasons. Here in North America, summer and winter are our inhales—our energetically slow periods. Spring and autumn are the exhales, bustling and filled with activity. The inhales and exhales of life are in rhythm with the seasons. When we live more attuned to these, we live in flow, better understanding the connectedness of all things. Nature gives us these cues to help guide us and teach us not only how to commune with it, but also with ourselves.

◄ The passage of time is never more evident than in the garden, even when you live in a place that does not exhibit the classic signs that usher us from one season to the next.

Summer's corn offering.

While there are four seasons in a year, there are two in the garden: the warm season is spring/summer, and the cool season is fall/winter. What I've learned, thanks to the garden, is that there can be individual days that embody the qualities of an entire season. Before dawn it's a cool 42°F (5.6°C), warming up into the seventies (twenties) for midday, and then getting chilly again in the evening. When I reflect on how this all began as an effort to be connected to nature—to be grounded to and by that—I smile, thinking about how different life is when you're outside long enough to experience all of her seasons in a single day.

So why does this matter, these seasons? They'll carry us through our days with a deeper joy, and eventually, when they're all stacked up on top of each other, they'll amount to traditions and nostalgia baked into our bones and into those of our children. As this book unfolds, I'll share how to seize the seasons and even extend them, as well as which plants do best in each of them. While our climates may be different, many of us can grow the same things, just perhaps at different times.

In one of the houses I grew up in, there was a huge wall of windows overlooking our horse pasture. On late stormy nights, I'd fall asleep to the sound of rain on the tin carport next to my bedroom. If lightning and thunder came, my mother would get out of bed, turn on the twinkle lights that she always had strung around the house in autumn and winter, wake me up, light candles, and make us hot chocolate with a little capful of peppermint schnapps. We would wrap ourselves in thick blankets and quietly watch the sky light up through those windows together. I realize now as an adult that this simple observance of nature, this cozy recollection of celebrating storm season—winter—has given me a forever love of rain and thunderstorms. I can smell them hours before they hit. And so can my children now, too.

As a gardener, I now realize how the negative ions in the rain rejuvenate. They clear the air, fill us with vitality, and visibly make our plants grow seemingly overnight. This is indeed something to honor, see, and touch.

As we have abandoned ritual and seasonal living with our busy modern lives, we have also forgotten about rest. We can overcome any detour with a digital map on our phones rerouting us. We can go to a coffee shop if our home's Wi-Fi is out. We can order dinner to be delivered if we aren't in the mood to cook. We can't be deterred or inconvenienced. Though I believe that, in order to live a real life, we must.

One summer, my husband and I took our family to stay in Central Tennessee for a month and we were stunned by all the summer storms. Being from Southern California for so long, we forgot what it was like to have unpredictable weather. We were relieved by it! We reveled in the delays caused by the storms. The world felt like it stopped during these torrential downpours because our attention was pushed outside. We'd find ourselves drawn to the porch to watch the lightning and listen to the rain. It would pass quickly, within fifteen minutes. We were rewired by those pauses in our days and could noticeably feel it soothe our systems. As we quickly discovered, we needed the breaks.

Pumpkins make fall feel cozy and festive. Because they can be used for meals, holiday decor, or overall autumnal moodiness, they are a garden must.

The seasons bring us back to center and engage our senses. If you find yourself a bit low and lost in your days, take a step back. Let the garden inspire you to reset and realign to the season. Commune with her. Later in these pages, I'll share my tips for gardening in all seasons as well as ways to connect through them, too.

Living Seasonally

Living seasonally simply means living in alignment with your seasons, taking the time to set new intentions with each new season, follow the pace of nature, and nourish yourself with what is locally available and in peak readiness. In a world where we have every convenience, it takes intentionality and planning to embrace and celebrate each season. Like dressing for the weather, there is a layering process I like to follow when planning out each season.

This is an exercise to help you get into the mood of the current season, whatever it may be. It helps orient your days and create balance with wherever you are in the seasonal cycle, and ultimately, with

the moon and where the earth is in orbit. From this 30,000-foot (9 km) view, you can then get more granular and set your eyes on how you want to spend your days within a given season.

At the start of each season, sit down and map out how you'll approach the coming months. Think about the current season and ask yourself these questions:

- What am I growing, foraging, and eating?
- What pace of life is the season holding?
- What holidays and traditions are to be celebrated?
- How can the rhythm of my days match the pace of nature?
- How can I engage my senses to align with the season?

For example, as autumn approaches (I'll use her as an example since she's my favorite), I'll sit down with a steaming cup of Earl Gray tea or maybe some hot cider, pull on some wool socks, and light an apple-scented candle. I'll immerse my senses in the coming season's delights and start to map out what the family has going on. Fall in America is traditionally marked by the business of back-to-school, a long Labor Day weekend, intense football games, a crafty Halloween, and a bountiful Thanksgiving.

School-aged children have so much going on this time of year and all the laziness of summer is whisked away. Now is a great time to complement the craziness with slow nature walks collecting fallen purple and yellow leaves. It's time to send the kids out to gather herbs for chili and stews. Setting aside a dedicated time for tea in the afternoons to reconnect, or a quiet hour with young children to help them reset before dinner, is a great way to keep the fast pace tempered.

As for the season's menu, autumn is where we get to lean into the warm season's harvest, complemented by the shoulder season before the first frost hits. Soups enter our family's rotation and we're finally using all those summer squash we've stored. Leafy greens are abundant and are being

There's nothing as delicious as a perfectly plump tomato warmed and ripened by the sun.

Summer calls for longer days outside, basking in the sun while we have it.

succession sown. Cauliflower and broccoli are being planted, while we're starting to dip into our saved jars of tomato marinara for classic spaghetti and meatballs.

The autumn equinox is a great time to think about hosting a dinner party or a gathering of friends to kick off the season. There's something about attending a seasonal event that sets a new tone for a family. It's an invisible anchor that shifts something within us. Additionally, inviting friends to experience how we use the garden is a part of what inspires them to take on their own gardening endeavors. I find that showcasing how we go from seed to table brings the kitchen garden to life. There is an additional love in being the friend that helps orient everyone back to nature, when I know I am the outlier who is turning her face to the sun for direction. There is no better way to help others connect than to invite them in.

In the autumn kitchen garden, there is a new beginning. A new set of seeds and crops has been started, all to complement the cool temperatures and a warming palette. Root crops are planted with the intent to overwinter them, and leafy greens and lettuces are brought into the fray. Protecting the soil and plants from the elements, while still using them to our advantage, is key. Fall gardening is marked by nets and hoops and garden bed covers to add warmth to the garden as needed, with a keen eye toward varieties that are fast to mature and slow to bolt in the early days after planting.

The season, the weather, and our distance from the sun inform what we can grow. What we grow informs what we'll eat and how we'll adorn our homes. This beautiful autumn dance brings appreciation and presence into our spirits, pushing us to celebrate with mulled wine while it's in season, thanks to the grapes and their vines. It has us making last-of-summer tomato sandwiches until we can't stomach them a moment more.

Every season can be like this. No shorter than need be and no longer than necessary. Just enough.

SOLSTICE AND EQUINOX IDEAS

WINTER SOLSTICE

The winter solstice is the longest night of the year, representing death and surrender as well as the oncoming welcoming of new and fresh light. Let go of the shadows in your life and mind and lean into the light.

· Make a yule log
· Light candles after the sun goes down and use them as your only source of light for the evening
· Make a wreath with foraged boughs and berries
· Drink dandelion root tea with cacao
· Set intentions for the coming year
· Watch the sunrise
· Drink mulled wine
· Do a cleanse of your home to get any negative energy and clutter out
· Stargaze and make an intention on a shooting star

SPRING EQUINOX

Spring represents the return of light and warmth. Rebirth and recommitment guide your intention setting, with a focus on gratitude and abundance for the oncoming season.

· Plant seeds
· Organize stagnant areas of your home
· Create a nature mandala
· Fill your home with fresh flowers
· Make a quiche and adorn it with herbs and flowers
· Decorate wooden eggs
· Go on a nature walk to find all the baby animals and fresh buds coming up from the soil
· Collect some flowers to press
· Enjoy foraging for nettle and drinking nettle tea with honey

SUMMER SOLSTICE

The brightest and longest day of the year warrants a bonfire deep into the night, sending the season's flowers ablaze in the flames as an offering to the coming season. Allow your routines to fall away as you embrace long, lazy days that gift you with a bit more time for languishing.

· Make flower crowns
· Gather with friends and family for a feast and bonfire
· Make a berry cobbler
· Take a long hike and picnic
· Make honey cakes
· Make sun tea with fresh herbs in cold water left out in the sun
· Take a bath filled with flowers
· Make lavender sachets for dream-inducing and catching
· Make a sun bread loaf

AUTUMN EQUINOX

The northern and southern hemispheres are experiencing the same day length, and the Earth is in balance just for a moment. The colder, slower, darker season is incoming, inspiring us to seize our moments and acknowledge our abundance with supreme gratitude.

· Hang and dry herbs
· Make beeswax candles to guide and illuminate as the darker days come
· Bake an apple pie
· Collect acorns and put them on display
· Gather fallen leaves and make a garland
· Create a new and balance-focused rhythm for your routine
· Assemble and drink fresh chai tea
· Host a harvest dinner
· Enjoy a simmer pot with apple, cinnamon, vanilla, and rosemary

ENGAGING OUR SENSES FOR THE SEASONS

A quick way to get in touch with the current season is to think about the five senses. Creating a sense of place in your home and nostalgia for all who enter it begins with the senses. Most notably, our olfactory system is so deeply tied to scent-memory that aligning moments in life with nature's rhythm doubly enforces joyful memories. Here are some ideas for unlocking each sense:

Engage **sight** with natural decor like dried leaf garlands and in-season floral arrangements. I love to pick a few flowers and put them by my children's beds as a sweet surprise. It's also fun to get out and collect things that speak to you. Gather fallen pinecones to place in a bowl, olive tree trimmings to add volume to a bouquet, and smoothed beach stones to pile up in the sink with a few drops of essential oil (a chic touch I learned while working at fancy hotels!).

For **scent**, try diffusing oils, making a simmer pot with herbs and flowers, or burning candles to waft life throughout the house. Don't forget that cooking your seasonal fare will achieve this, too. Nothing beats coming home from a football game to the smell of chili on the stove.

As for **touch**, updating the house with linens in the warm season, flannels in the cold, and some silk in between can help us lean into the physical element of a season. Change bedding and clothing out each season for this reason and for practicality. Storing puffy and shearling jackets and bringing out the breezy dresses is a great practice to not only simplify your wardrobe, but to keep you present at the moment of summer's arrival.

Taste is the easiest sense to unlock, especially when meals align with the kitchen garden's offerings. Supplement your kitchen from local sources when the garden is either late to develop or lacks ingredients that are hard to grow. Think about ways to weave garden-fresh ingredients into each meal of the day, as well as ways to use all your kitchen skills via roasting, baking, grilling, or juicing.

A potato leek pie perfectly celebrates the fall season.

Lastly, **sound** is a great reminder of the season. Our family loves having playlists that tie to memories. We even have special songs that are just for when we get in the car to go to the beach or when we go to get our Christmas tree. We play a lot of Celtic music in autumn, fun and fresh beach songs in summer, and cozy jazz in winter. There's something fun about saving certain music or albums for a specific time of year.

The more you challenge yourself to bring the garden to life inside your home, the more you'll find yourself building the garden around that desire. I now grow things like strawflower to make wreaths to hang around the house, and I love to grow lemongrass for decoration as much as for cooking. Nature inspiring life and life inspiring nature. It's full circle.

▶ Lavender is a great herb for many things, including simmer pots, sachets, and even simple syrups.

Our Seasons in the Kitchen Garden

As previously mentioned, there are two distinct seasons in the garden: a cool season and a warm season. Although, those two seasons might not always line up exactly with the calendar. If you're somewhere with a very mild climate, like Southern California, you may not feel those distinct seasons as much as a gardener in a more temperate region. In fact, we live about two months adjusted from the rest of the United States, not feeling any sort of cool weather until winter has already been on the calendar for a month. When thinking about the garden and planting, consider your cool season and the warm season.

Most edible plants prefer either cool or warm temperatures for germination and growing. Since each region is a bit different, instead of using spring/summer and fall/winter to guide you, use warm and cool season as the guides. I've learned to ignore many traditional planting calendars and guides and instead reference the temperature each plant needs to thrive for determining when to start the seeds.

I will never forget one April day heading down to a local nursery I frequent and perusing the tomato aisle for seedlings to plant out that day. There was an older man working there who was watching me out of the corner of his eye.

"Excuse me, sir, do you have any tomato recommendations?" I asked him, curious about which varieties he liked.

"None until we hit nighttime temperatures above the mid-fifties (about 13°C)." he responded. My eyes lit up. This was the wisdom I had been looking for! We chatted for quite a while, and I eventually learned his favorite tomato varieties, as well as which tomatoes won local taste-testing awards. He also told me why I might want to avoid the fancy, fun-named hybrids. They lack flavor, even if they do look pretty.

Although the aisles of that nursery were full of greenhouse-started tomato plants, it was still too cold for them to really thrive in the garden. I now use that info as a guide for my warm-season garden. Late April typically proves to be a great time for me to start the plants that like hot weather. For you, late April might be too soon, or perhaps too late. The better target is the man's advice to wait until nighttime temperatures are above the mid-fifties (about 13°C), instead of relying on the date showing on the calendar.

For cool-season plants I grow in autumn and winter, I find getting the seeds germinated in September allows the plants to have the benefit of soil and air warmth to get going, but then they slow their growth as the temperatures fall. This is especially beneficial for crops like brassicas, broccoli, and cauliflower, where the vegetable we eat is actually the flower bud. The gorgeous white florets of a cauliflower are undeveloped flower buds,

Tomatoes waiting for more sun to ripen.

One weekend's worth of a warm-season harvest.

and we don't want the plant to go to flower and seed (a process called bolting) too soon or we'll miss out on the edible part of the plant. Timing your planting right and hitting the cold temperatures properly ensures that your cauliflower plants don't bolt.

Similarly, early spring's timing is about making sure you can germinate your seeds yet steer clear of frost. A mini or large greenhouse can help here. Ideal timing will have your seedlings developing with the warm weather and long days, and your peak harvest should occur at the end of summer.

COMMON WARM-SEASON AND COOL-SEASON VEGETABLES

Warm-season plants: tomatoes, peppers, squash, zucchini, beans, corn, cucumbers, eggplant, zinnias, sunflowers, okra, melons

Cool-season veggies: broccoli, cauliflower, Asian greens, leafy greens and lettuces, potatoes, carrots, beets, onions, garlic, peas, radicchio, swiss chard, radish

Bringing Foraging into the Fold

As a child, my stepfather would take me on hikes in Yosemite National Park and point out the flora and fauna as we went along. At the time it was to share his own interest and knowledge, but also most likely to drown out my whining about hiking. All I remember as a kid about hiking was how much I didn't like the outfit, but now, as an adult, I'd kill to go on a hike at any given moment with my stepdad, Den.

Somehow, the nuggets of wisdom about wild edible plants from my stepfather stuck with me, and now I am absolutely enthralled by the magic of the free food growing all around us! How exciting is that? Even now, when I spot elderflower blooming all over Southern California, I look around thinking, "No one even knows how magical this tree is! They're just walking by it, like it's no big deal." The art of foraging has been long lost due to simply not needing to hunt and gather anymore. Instead, we shop.

However, a great way to get back into touch with the seasons is to go foraging and create a personal archive or map of your local haunts. Keep a foraging map or journal to help you recall what, when, and where your local wild food supplies are. For example, in our neighborhood, there are prickly pears, elderflowers and elderberries, cattails, dandelions, cress, wild celery, and more. Without my foraging map or journal, it's hard to recall when they're blooming and all the nooks and crannies where we find them.

To be most specific, print out a map of your local area and either directly annotate on it or use tracing paper to create a new map that outlines the main streets and landmarks, adding in notes about where you find your natural treasures. Include the month, cross streets, and other notable plants or buildings nearby. Be sure to note

A simple foraging map serves as a reminder of what is growing where.

Out foraging for prickly pear with the kids.

Identifying wild fennel and getting to know its smell and feel.

if there are multiple locations of a single plant. Year over year, if you see a decrease in the plant's population, you'll know to stop sourcing from that site. Likewise, if you see an increase in a particular forageable plant, you may be able to take home a bit more.

The rules for foraging:

1. Absolutely do not eat or apply anything to your body that you are unsure of. A "maybe" is a "no" when it comes to foraging.

2. Give an offering. A song, a prayer of gratitude, or some native seeds will do. This is based on the laws of reciprocity that nature follows.

3. Do not take from the first plant you see. Be sure there is more than just one plant. Ideally, there are many sources of forageable goods.

4. Take only a third, if not less, of what is available.

5. Be sure you'll use what you collect.

FOR THE LITTLE ONES

To keep children occupied on foraging adventures, create a scavenger hunt for them. Print pictures of some local flora and fauna, and have the little ones check things off as they find them. Additionally, have the kids bring a notebook and pencil and collect specimens to draw while you're out in the field or back at home.

Modern conveniences make us feel like we can purchase anything we need, but there are nutrient-packed plants like dandelion and nettle that are readily available all around us for free. They draw us out into nature and back to our roots. Often, we can't even find plants like these "over the counter," whereas in nature there are an abundance of options from summer to winter. I also find local and native flowers and plants make the most stunning and authentic arrangements for the house. Whether it's a centerpiece on the dining table or a garland above the fireplace, there's something so fun and unexpected about seeing a natural treasure being honored inside a home.

As you learn to live and play within nature's guidelines, you will quickly be enchanted by the beauty of co-creating within those natural boundaries. Tomatoes become sweeter when enjoyed only at their peak and not forced to ripen artificially throughout the year. Peach juice running down your chin, a cup of steaming hot tea after a windy autumn hike, the crunchy sound of the first fallen leaves, the glittering snow in the sun; these are moments to cherish and revel in when they are presently around you.

The kitchen garden reminds you of this again and again. It keeps you engaged with the seasons as they unfold, as they come alive and then fade away. Enjoy the rhythm and pace that nature has set. The pace of modern life isn't quite meant for enjoying the seasons or for the gift of presence, but the garden tethers you to both.

FORAGEABLES

Here are some of my favorite forageables in the Northern Hemisphere by their season of availability.

SPRING
Nettle
Morel mushrooms
Miner's lettuce

FALL
Dandelion root
Rosehips
Elderberries
Chanterelles

SUMMER
Elderflower
Yarrow
Berries
Mullein

WINTER
Wood sorrel
Acorns
Crab apples
Pine

In the garden, our awareness is heightened. The need to dance within the tiles of the ballroom floor that is the stretch of days between the last frost of spring and the first frost of fall becomes our focus. While traditional holidays embody some elements of celebrating what's in season, it's on our shoulders to turn an awareness to the path of the changing sun as an indicator of how to speed up or slow down our lives, rather than turning the page of a calendar.

▶ Nothing compares to in-season ingredients whether grown in the garden or foraged from the land.

CHAPTER 2

PLAN

There is no time quite as exciting as that leading up to a new growing season in the garden. We get to dream and doodle about how we want to bring the garden to life. Think of the garden as an extension of the home; it's another room that sits just outside. Each season should hold a purpose and feel a certain way, all while aiming to be as efficient and useful as possible. Each garden bed has a calling, with form and function blending in harmony.

The way a garden looks is often a reflection of the gardener themselves. Some like very tidy gardens and some like a wild tangle. My personal style is a blend of both. I like to have a somewhat wild border around the garden, beckoning pollinators and tumbling into the pathways. But within my garden beds, I prefer a sense of symmetry and architecture, especially once the plants are established and mature. There is a particular aesthetic I like to achieve, being that I want the garden to really beckon both you and me out there. There have been many days when I wander outside to harvest for dinner and see the neighbors having a barbecue, yet half the guests are peeking through the fence with their cocktails in hand, surveying my garden.

Though I have a specific style, which I'll teach you about in a bit, I want to encourage you to test and trial what feels good in your space. My life changed the day I started growing my own food. It changes not only in all the accomplishment of tasks or health benefits achieved, but in the act of

being able to learn again, to build intuition and know-how from scratch, and to build confidence. I could freely fail and succeed in a way that was fun and useful and taught me something I had forgotten about, which was, in essence, how to play.

It was total destiny in that the very first gardening book I read was about a version of intensive gardening. I was visiting my father out of state while he was undergoing cancer treatments. One of the last healthy memories I have of him is walking around the charming downtown of St. George, Utah. He and I both loved to peruse used bookstores, so we sauntered in and pulled out corners of books to read their titles, maybe grabbing one off the shelf if it so deserved the honor. A book titled *Postage Stamp Gardening* grabbed *me*, I swear. Written in the 1970s, the author used a mix of organic, biodynamic, and high-intensity gardening to dispel the idea that we need long, neat, widely spaced rows of crops. The author encouraged planting things much closer together, in companion with beneficial plants and flowers and with the goal of growing a lot of food in a small space. I started out with two raised beds, and since I needed to feed as many people as possible from them, I learned by trial and error when it came to planning out a garden that was functional and productive. To this day, I garden in alignment with the principles I learned in that book combined with the experience I now have. I know now when to keep, bend, or break the rules, but I didn't always. Eventually, you too will have a ton of techniques to utilize in the garden, but none better than your own experience.

◀ A bird's eye view of my garden in San Juan Capistrano with ten raised beds and a limestone fountain at the center.

Setting Up Your Garden

The original kitchen gardens date back to the fifteenth century and were (and still are) commonly called *potagers* in France. They were right outside the door to the kitchen (hence the name) and were a mixture of vegetables, herbs, and flowers, all for use by the cook. Around the world, people throughout history have worked their land to create functional gardens. In North America, it became common for the female head of farming households to turn about an acre of land into a kitchen garden for feeding the family. Eventually, in the United States, urbanites and suburbanites alike planted and grew Victory gardens in the 1940s to support World War II efforts. Victory gardens ranged from a sizeable one acre down to tiny backyard postage-stamp gardens, all supported by gardening knowledge delivered via the U.S. government. While this speaks to the history of kitchen gardening, it also speaks to the fact that, no matter the size of the space you have, a bountiful food garden is in your future—with a little planning, of course.

If you've not yet set up your garden space, there are some "rules of thumb" to help the process, as well as some ideas for getting started. Location is everything, and the ideal garden placement for gardeners in the Northern Hemisphere is south facing, as it gets the most sun exposure throughout the day. In the Southern Hemisphere, north-facing is best. This is not a deal-breaker, but this target orientation might dictate whether you clear out a space or choose somewhere else. Perhaps more importantly, be sure the space gets a minimum of six hours of sun each day. This is not negotiable if you want to grow fruiting vegetables like tomatoes, peppers, cucumbers, and sun-loving flowers. Some edible plants are okay with just four hours of sun, but you'd be limiting yourself. If you need to go into the front yard, up on a balcony, or to a community garden to access more sunlight, do that.

Plant densely and with diversity.

Another location note is to think about the accessibility of the garden. Convenience makes a more successful gardener, and kitchen gardens are often close to the kitchen for that reason. They make cooking from the garden easy. Additionally, be sure there is a water source available. At least one hose bib is necessary. If you don't have a water access point close by, install one, or find a way to add automatic irrigation that's buried so you won't trip over it.

MEASURING YOUR SPACE

Decide where to place your garden based on the location of any buildings to consider that cast shade. Then, begin to measure out your space. You'll want a measuring tape and potentially some stakes and twine to aid in visualizing the garden beds.

For in-ground gardening, this tends to be easier. However, in-ground garden beds can have beautiful edging details like shallow bricks or steel. You want to identify the shapes and sizes of your beds, as well as pathways.

To properly measure the space, you will need to know the perimeter, as well as the distance from each side to the other. I like to establish a central focal point for the garden, so that I can align my beds in relation to that point. Sometimes a central spot is just a plot on the map, or sometimes it's a fountain or sitting area. You get to decide.

On a lot that's less than one-quarter of an acre (0.10 hectare), it's easy for the garden to be close to the kitchen.

Using a grid to map this out and see how the garden is shaped and positioned is helpful. In fact, it's a must. Use graph paper to create your space on paper, and then all the other pieces will fall into place. I like to have each cell represent a square foot. You can use a scale ruler that has three sides to help you create a measurement ratio if your garden is large and you need to adjust the scale on paper.

Using your measurements, you can see how much room you have for things like pathways, borders, and beds. More on that next.

IRRIGATION

Ideally, each raised bed has its own hose bib, coming up from the inside of the bed via PVC pipe. This is important to think about before any building occurs. Position your irrigation up against the edge of a raised bed to protect it. It is a good idea to dig trenches below where your garden will be so that the irrigation can be hidden underground. I prefer to use soaker hoses, but drip irrigation is a great option as well. While sprinklers are also fine, it is the roots, not the leaves, of the plant that need water. I find that sprinklers leave more room for mildew and sunburn. Soaker hoses are moveable and don't clog as much. Be sure to measure

them out as they will be laying—typically in an *S* shape, or a circular manner. They often come in 25- or 50-foot (8 or 15.5 m) options.

Lastly, hand watering is still of course a great option! The downfall here is a lack of control. It's harder to tell how much you're watering and is very time-consuming. Arguably, time well spent. My garden does better with irrigation, but my mind does better with hand watering. Think about it.

RAISED BEDS VS. IN-GROUND PLANTING

Once you have your location chosen, you then need to decide if you're going to plant at ground level or in raised beds. The benefits of gardening in-ground are its inexpensive cost and, if your native soil is healthy, the ability to garden as true to nature as possible. It's much easier to have small pathways with in-ground gardens as well, because you just need a space wide enough for a wheelbarrow tire to get through the foliage. With raised beds, keep in mind immovable structures. To maneuver a wheelbarrow through, you need wider pathways between them.

The benefits of gardening in raised beds include the ability to control the soil, the simplicity of managing pests, and the ease of physically managing the garden because you aren't on your hands and knees or squatting to tend your space. However, raised beds can be more costly.

There is also an aesthetic to consider. Many people build raised beds, whether out of stone, wood, or wattle, simply because they like how it looks and the character it creates in companionship with the home. If you're building a new garden and want it to be a certain aesthetic or perhaps "designed," begin by evaluating the design style of your house. When a home's exterior design style matches the garden's design style, the garden becomes an enhancing element for the property. For example, traditional-, colonial-, and craftsman-style homes are complemented well by wooden raised beds. More historic or stately

An 18-inch (46-cm)-high redwood raised bed with a cap trim for sitting on.

Sunflowers in the garden's borders attract pollinators, are edible, and make amazing cut flowers.

homes, perhaps with a European influence, look fantastic with stone raised beds or with in-ground gardens that have a willow wattle or steel edging surrounding them. If you have a stucco house, perhaps consider cinderblock raised beds covered in plaster or go with a more rustic aluminum raised bed.

PATHWAYS

Once you've found your location and decided whether you'll garden in-ground or in raised beds, it's time to draw out a map and use those measurements you have. In doing so, you'll create pathways and create a configuration for your beds. The decided size of your garden's pathways is personal preference. When gardening in-ground, I prefer small pathways to maximize space and allow myself larger passageways once things mature. Tomatoes can get tangled if you let them, and it could cause the entire garden to divulge into chaos. For in-ground gardens, I prefer a minimum width of 2 feet (61 cm). For raised beds, 3 feet (91 cm) is the minimum width to get a wheelbarrow through for amending soil and pulling out plants.

Next, think about what materials to use to make your pathways. This is more of a consideration for raised-bed gardens or if the gardener is going for a fully designed space. Some common choices are pea gravel (my personal favorite), decomposed granite (DG), gravel, brick or pavers, grass, and mulch. Some folks use straw or cardboard, especially with an in-ground garden, and that works too. Cost is always a consideration, so plain ol' dirt is a great choice as well; just know you'll have more weeds to contend with. When choosing a pathway material, consider whether your chosen medium gets hot, drains well, and stays tidy over time. DG can look nice but gets muddy, and it can be painful on bare feet. Pea gravel can get messy and displaced, and bricks can be hot. Weigh the pros and cons for your family and go from there.

Pathways do in fact serve another important role in the garden; they are barriers and borders. Pathways should be free of weeds, and they are useful for stopping the potential spread of weeds from one planting bed to the next or from the lawn into a planting bed. A good pathway plan is especially important if you're working with in-ground beds that don't have built edges.

◄ Pea gravel pathways with flagstone steppingstones allow us to be barefoot or wear our fancy Ruby Slippers in the garden.

BORDERS

An element of British gardens I picked up from watching hours of Monty Don's *Gardeners' World* while nursing my youngest son is that all gardens have magnificent borders around the garden's exterior—big, booming edges along fences or all around a space. And for good reason—they are lush and stunning, but also purposeful in drawing in pollinators. Pollinator borders and strips are planting areas designed to bring the good pollinators in and keep the pests out. The idea is to add pollen- and nectar-centric plants to as large of a space as possible, so that the bees, butterflies, birds, and other beneficial creatures can cross the garden on their way from one part of the strip to another. If you can reserve space in your garden to add a few feet of flower border around the edges, the garden will shine.

In the practice of permaculture—and of course in nature itself— borders are there to bring in or keep out certain elements. Permaculturists use a concept known as *rings of use* where the most frequented places, such as food gardens and chicken coops, are kept close to the home. Places on a property that people don't need to frequent as often, such as flower borders or pastures, can be further away from the home. Kitchen gardeners can also use this concept to get granular in deciding where things go. Kitchen gardens are at their best when they're right off the kitchen and mapped out to have the most-used plants closest to the door. Because kitchen gardeners are always rotating the plants in the garden, and the entire space is typically manageable at the home garden scale, this is less important than it is on a farm. However, rings of use can come into play as you build out your garden to include borders and surrounding foliage. Consider dedicating space for plants that draw in pollinators around the borders of your kitchen garden. See page 88 for more on permaculture concepts that are useful in the kitchen garden.

GARDEN BED CONFIGURATION AND DESIGN

Here is where we start to assemble all the principles just discussed. I started by coming up with a design configuration and bed sizes. Classic rectangular garden beds are just fine, but if you want more of that French potager look, adding some square beds or perhaps *L*-shaped beds can make the space feel more intentional, like a room.

If your garden space is straightforward, for example just a big rectangle, then you have a lot of flexibility and can create a unique configuration, perhaps making each of the four corners an *L*-shaped bed, with some square beds within that. If your garden is a less common shape (I once had a triangular plot of land), then it can be most eye-pleasing to have a lot of order in a simple configuration.

Some common bed shapes are rectangles, squares, *L*-shaped, *U*-shaped, keyhole beds that are like squares with a small space cut out for you to access, triangles, and circles. Play around with each shape in your space, within the confines of your garden. From there, add in those pathways

The garden in full bloom with our limestone fountain.

ADDING DESIGN ELEMENTS

Once the bones of the garden are in place, we can play a bit and add some fun. One of the favorite features of our home garden is our functional fairy door. I had it built into one of the raised beds with a waterproof box and a door that opens and closes. The goal was to add something fun for children to stumble upon. I often hide things in the fairy door for the kids to find, adding some everyday magic into their lives. This also played into my hope for the garden to be a place my kids yearned for and felt called to. We also added brass number plates to the garden beds, which help me keep track of which bed is which and allow others to help me, and it looks pretty, too. These tiny details take the garden up a level and give the space a captivating feeling of thoughtfulness and enchantment.

Another way to make a garden sing is with a water feature. The sound of water running is one of the most soothing noises to hear, fading into the background with an imperceptible calming effect. A bird bath is another option, giving a critical water source to pollinators and bringing in wildlife.

and borders. If you have limited space, it may help to place borders first, or to forego them altogether.

As you play with the garden shapes, keep in mind where you will be viewing the garden from the outside. Professional landscape designers call these *sight lines*. because they are where your line of sight is. You will want to look at the garden in a way that guides you into it. This creates access points, like where there is a break in the raised beds, where you place a garden gate, where trellises or arches go, and how the overall layout is designed in relation to your ability to see the garden well.

I often have about three different design configurations with different bed shapes and different features, to help me decide how to use the land. I have seen stunning kitchen gardens designed with a table at the center for outdoor dining or even four simple circular beds surrounded by a square border. Let your creativity run wild and think deeply about the use of the space. It is meant to be practical and grow for maximum yield, or will you be out there entertaining? These are great questions to ask yourself so that you have a space that is, above all, used.

My stepfather made this garden bench out of my childhood bed and it's the perfect touch of nostalgia and charm.

Statues and sitting areas are an additional way to add personality and give people something to "find" while moseying about in the garden. Again, matching the aesthetic of your home is a great approach to take when choosing these accessories, but whatever brings you joy is good enough. The additional whimsy and personal touch they provide adds so much character to a space. Benches and small tables and chairs positioned perfectly for admiring a certain plant, or situated somewhere unexpected, can make the garden even more of a room instead of just a plot of land with veggies growing on it.

With the garden's location, beds, pathways, and borders accounted for, you now have a garden design achieved. The added element of a water feature and some personalized touches makes the entire endeavor feel intentional as opposed to just having popped up out of nowhere. After these decisions are made, it's time to move on to choosing plants and creating a strategy for the two vegetable growing seasons, the cool season and the warm season.

Cloches are protective coverings, often woven with natural materials. They are a great way to protect small plants, but also add character to your space.

Choosing Your Plants

When planning what plants you're going to grow in the garden, there should be a hierarchy in place, seeing as most of us only have a certain amount of land to work with. Let the limits guide you but learn to bend the rules by planting vertically and over a longer growing season than you think you might have. When it comes to the business of choosing plants, there is a method to the madness.

To prepare yourself for the many gardening years ahead of you, one crucial piece of knowledge will be getting to know the ins and outs of your climate. In the United States, we have something called *hardiness zones* that are established by the U.S. Department of Agriculture to break the country up into sections based on the growing climate in each zone. Cold-climate gardeners in the north have a lower growing zone, while those in the warmer south have higher growing zone numbers. All fruits and vegetables have a preference in where they're grown, so getting to know which plants are best for your climate will help you have success, especially if they are winter-hardy plants that can live for many years. Most vegetable crops are grown as annual plants only meant to live in

FOR THE LITTLE ONES

With each garden comes the potential for new surprises and moments of delight for children. Our fairy door in one of the raised beds allows us to hide treasures inside for the children. Every so often I'll hide a little wooden toy or some treats, and the kids will either find them naturally when they're drawn to the garden to poke around, or I'll mention that I heard a little chime coming from the garden. They'll go running outside in search of the fairy's treasure. It's just a little trick to create some magic in the garden, but it's also a sneaky-mom trick to get my kids to be outside with me.

◄ The famous fairy door.

our gardens for a single growing season. The zones come into play for these plants in determining their ideal planting time, which we'll talk more about in a later chapter. If you have questions, ask the nursery closest to your home for some guidance. Each of our gardens is its own microclimate. Some of us may live on a hill, in a valley, at a greater elevation, or perhaps near the sea. Each of these things can slightly alter the general climate of our garden.

The very first step in choosing which plants to grow is thinking about your goals for the season. Some years you may be looking to replace the produce aisle of the grocery store entirely, and others, perhaps you're just wanting to learn to how to grow a new vegetable or some flowers. The goals dictate how seriously you take the garden mapping process and the quantity of each plant you grow. Most vegetable gardens have space limitations, so you must decide what gets the most space based on how much of the plant you will consume. To make this process easier, I created a useful planting system.

I use a technique I call *poker planting* to categorize plants, using the value of the cards in a game of poker to represent my plant priorities: Aces, Faces, Plains, and Jokers. Aces are either used as a high or a low in card games, but here we're using them as the ultimate high card. Faces are the Kings, Queens, and Jacks—high scoring cards (but secondary to the Aces). Plains are the normal 2, 3, 4, and so on up to 10 cards that are used in general play. Jokers are the extras—typically used as a wild card in many games. Categorizing your plants within the buckets of our poker system helps keep priorities in mind, so we aren't planting tons of cute little cucamelons instead of something useful that we eat a lot of, like potatoes. Even the best-intentioned gardener will get caught up in the novelty and excitement of a new variety of snacking tomato, quick to forget their

◀ Corn, tomatoes, herbs, peppers, and cucumbers.

Planning what to grow starts with the end in mind. What do you want to harvest?

dreams of stocking the pantry with marinara for the year.

I used to describe this poker planting process differently, using an old business concept. Stephen Covey, a well-known businessman, used to talk about planning and prioritizing your life. He would have people visualize their lives like an empty glass jar that gets filled up with the tasks and doings of life. He tells you to think of your big priorities as big rocks, your less important goals as pebbles, and the least value-driven components as sand. If you fill up your jar first with sand, it will be filled with nonimportant tasks and events, leaving less room for the big priorities; but, if you place your big rocks in first followed by your pebbles, you get a jar full of the most important things. You can then pour the sand into the cracks, allowing your attention to fall on the most value-centric elements first and foremost. In the end, you still get to squeeze in the little fun moments. Keeping the big things in focus is what leads to a fulfilled life.

The garden is no different. At the start of every growing season this visual comes to mind because it's perfectly accurate. We need to choose what our priority plants are, plant them first, and then fill in the gaps with less-necessary plants.

POKER PLANTING CATEGORIES

Aces

Aces are the most important plants in your garden. These are vegetables you like and use the most and want to stop buying at the grocery store. These are the plants we allow to take up the most space in the garden and keep in the garden the longest. For example, I always grow garlic. It takes eight to nine months to grow, so it's using up space in my raised bed for most of the year, inhibiting me from using that space for a 120-day crop like squash. However, we use garlic constantly in the kitchen. It's quite versatile as you can use it raw, sauteed, or dried into a powder. You can even give it as a hostess gift or share it with neighbors. Garlic also keeps well in storage and has a myriad of health benefits. This is an ace for me. It checks all the boxes and therefore gets to take up as much time and space as it needs.

Faces

Faces are big players in the garden and will be filling in a lot of space. Even if you can't grow enough to replace what you buy at the store, that's okay. In our garden, these are crops like cucumbers and broccoli. We eat a ton of these, but they often take up a lot of space so I can't grow enough to entirely replace what we purchase from the store.

Plains

Plains are plants we love to grow and are often companions to the primary vegetables. Flowers and herbs fit into this group. This is also where we include radishes, scallions, carrots, beets, and other plants that are lovely, easy to sneak in anywhere, and enhance our meals immensely. I also consider my pollinator plants, which are vital to the garden's productivity, as add-ins here. They can be tucked in most anywhere or used to decorate the garden.

Reviewing last year's notes in my garden journal.

Jokers

Jokers are for fun! These plants are great to share, to test out, and to grow just because you're curious. Fill empty spots with these and tuck them into odd spaces. Each season, I choose a few jokers that I want to try, like scarlet runner beans or ground cherries. Eggplant fell into this category one year and now they've moved up to be something we grow each year in the Plains category.

As you make your lists of what you want to grow, I recommend doing a brain dump of every single plant you're drawn to or that you eat or use. Then go in and categorize which level of importance they each have. Remember, we need a mix to create a thriving ecosystem (and an exciting poker game!), so plan to include a bit of everything.

This system also helps us understand the return on investment (ROI) for our plants. If we use an entire bed for potatoes, but those are a huge main crop for the family, then it's worth the space and time investment and the sacrifice of not being able to grow something else there. Even with dense planting schemes, there's always an ROI for each different plant. Thinking through how much each vegetable contributes toward your overall goal makes each decision easier.

PLANTS PER PERSON

The last consideration when it comes to choosing plants is how many of each plant you're going to grow. To best know the expected yield of each plant, do a little research based on the variety of the vegetable. Some varieties are big producers, while others give you fewer but larger-sized goodies. I have a list below of some popular veggies and an approximation of how many plants are required per person per growing season. Multiply that by the number of people in your family and you have the loose number of plants you should grow. If you know your family eats a lot of sweet potatoes, increase the number of plants or research if there are special high-yielding varieties to include in your garden. Consider going through your grocery receipts or making a sample list of what you buy each week from the store to help curate what you plant and how much to grow.

Number of Plants Needed per Person

Artichokes: 1 plant
Arugula: 5 plants
Beans (bush): 6 plants
Beans (pole): 5 plants
Beets: 5 plants
Broccoli: 6–10 plants
Brussels sprouts: 2 plants
Cabbage: 2–4 plants
Carrots: 20 plants
Celery: 6 plants
Corn: 10–12 plants
Cucumber: 3 plants
Eggplant: 2 plants
Garlic: 10–15 cloves
Kale: 4 plants
Leek: 10 plants
Lettuce (leaf): 3 plants
Lettuce (head): 4 plants
Melon: 1–2 plants
Onion: 12–20 sets
Peas: 15–20 plants
Pepper: 3–5 plants
Potato: 10 plants
Spinach: 10 plants
Squash (summer): 1–2 plants
Squash (winter): 1–2 plants
Tomato (cherry): 2 plants
Tomato (sauce): 2 plants
Tomato (slicing): 2–4 plants

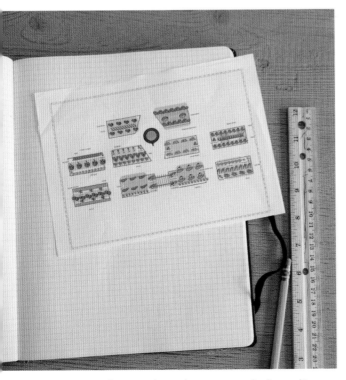

Every year I map out the garden on paper and online, making several edits as I go.

Designing Where It All Goes

Mapping out garden beds one-and-a-half seasons at a time is my practice. My godmother, Aunty Pammy, on the other hand, maps her whole year all at once. I can't do that because I have a hard time sticking to something so logical and am always reserving some room for the next season to tell *me* what *it* wants. Regardless of the extent of your planning, the basic premise lies in mapping things out while also thinking ahead to the next season and what is best primed for the next round of planting. Depending on where you live, that could just be a late sowing of a handful of crops, or it could be a full-on additional season in which you can grow anything and everything.

I use the term *designing* when planning my garden because there is an element of both aesthetics and science when it comes to placing your plants. With the poker planting system, we choose which plants we want and how many to grow. Next, we must map it all out. My exact process begins with a piece of graph paper and a pencil and ruler. I sit down and draw out my garden, using each graph square to represent either 1 or 2 square feet (930–1,860 cm²). I draw in the bed outlines and permanent trellises and structures and then start to tackle placing the Aces in the garden.

Here's where things get fun. The most important plants get placed first, as well as anything that climbs a trellis or hangs over a bed's edge, since we need them to be somewhere specific. Next, we add the Faces in and consider what companions go where.

The Poker Planting process is all about layering your plants based on priority and space. Once the Aces and trellising plants are in, then add your Faces and really try to fill in the garden with the Plains. Think more about planting in clumps than in rows. A full garden doesn't have room for weeds and confuses pests. Gardens with rows and rows of solitary plants make it nice and easy for elements

Mapping out the season's plants always starts with pencil to paper.

like wind and hail to wreak havoc, as well as for pests like cabbage moths to come in and lay eggs all over, creating tiny green caterpillars that eat all the cabbages, cauliflowers, and kale. Clumps of plants create biodiversity blocks and fill the space well with thriving and more resilient plants. Your clumps will start to become like circles of friends. Think of it as a series of bullseyes with the Ace in the middle and the other types surrounding it (see the Sample Planting Plan on page 49).

Another option is to start with a row of Aces plants and then stagger them, making a zigzag pattern as opposed to a straight row. Then add in staggered rows of your Faces and Plains. The less linear, the better. Always start by placing the largest plants first, and then see how much you can fit around them. While you may have room for just six radishes in a row alongside some broccoli and onions, you'll find that you can double that number if you instead break them up and sneak four sets of three radishes each around the onions. Do this in each bed, breaking crops up as needed so they are spread throughout the garden as opposed to in just one bed or one area. While this might feel harder at the time of planning, it makes for a more bountiful harvest and a diverse garden that is full of life.

In this warm-season garden, the Aces are tomatoes and basil. The Faces are carrots and onions, and the Plains are sage and thyme. The Jokers are colorful flowers along the garden's border.

Once all the plants are down on your paper and have a place in the garden, don't be afraid to move them around a bit to create some visual interest, if you haven't already. A garden that beckons you in is one that includes views and dimensions. Placing the tall plants in back and on the southern side not only creates visual appeal and draws your eye through the entire garden, but it also ensures that a little shade is created. Yes, in some instances you *do* want to create shade. On the other hand, if you don't want shade, place taller plants on the northern side. It's also possible to place the taller plants in the center of the bed, with some bushy fillers to encircle them, and then include vining plants to spill over edges. The possibilities are endless!

GARDEN COMPANIONS

Companion planting is a beautiful and important aspect of gardening. There are plants that complement each other and plants that steal nutrients from each other. Making sure the companions we are planting together are good for each other takes some research and practice, but you'll get the hang of it quickly. There are some general rules that make a big difference: garlic with beans and peas is a no-go. However, garlic and roses are beautiful together. Peas and carrots thrive with each other, as do tomatoes and basil. Cucumbers prosper with dill, and carrots love to be encircled by chives or leeks to keep carrot flies away. Additionally, companion plants can be used to attract or deter insects as needed. Plants that attract pests are called *trap plants*. They're the sacrificial lamb of the garden and are planted for the purpose of either being eaten first, thereby luring pests away from other desirable plants, or bringing in pollinators and other good bugs throughout the season.

Nasturtiums are my favorite companion plant. They're entirely edible from seed and stem to petal and leaf, with a peppery flavor. There are tons of different colored varieties, and they have a unique leaf. These plants make great borders or corner plants for adding color and symmetry, but nasturtiums also attract aphids. They can be a trap crop for things like brassicas that would otherwise be overrun with aphids. Nasturtiums are beauty and brawn together, with the highest return on investment a plant can give—and I quite like that.

ADDING FLOWERS TO THE MIX

I find that adding decorative and edible flowers creates some fantastic symmetry and borders in our beds. They also serve a purpose as companions and throw color into the mix. Every garden bed or row in my garden has flowers in it, no exceptions. They bring value and make the garden feel the most alive.

Favorite flowers for the vegetable garden:

- **Sunflowers** are a fantastic edible and a great companion plant. They also decontaminate the soil they're in, drawing up toxins.
- **Borage** is an edible flower with a cucumber taste. Its large foliage makes a great home for good bugs, and they are fantastic paired with tomatoes to attract pollinators.
- **Nasturtium** are a fabulous trap plant, distracting aphids from other crops, and they're entirely edible. They create fabulous borders and can hang over your bed's edge. Nasturtiums are well-loved by pollinators thanks to their flower shape.
- **Marigold** has an off-putting scent for many pests and is often planted with basil and tomatoes. They're edible as well, with petals that bake nicely.
- **Snapdragons** create some fun height in the garden and are also edible! They come in many colors and add a fun design element.
- **Yarrow** is fantastic for borders and for medicinal uses, plus it's a pollinator favorite.
- **Strawflower** dries beautifully and adds fun pops of color.

Sunflowers make beautiful border plants, create privacy, help nourish the soil, and trap pests.

Marigolds are planted with the tomatoes in my garden as a pest repellent.

Calendula acting as a trap plant for aphids.

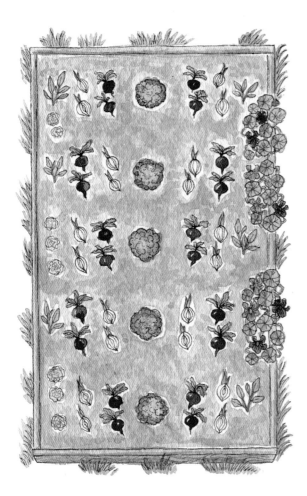

TERMS TO REMEMBER

Succession sowing is the act of sowing seeds of the same crop successively over the course of seven to fourteen days so that you have a consistent harvest of that crop. As you are harvesting some of your vegetables, you could also be sowing another round of those same seeds, while a third round of those veggies are already halfway to maturity.

Intercropping is the act of growing multiple species of edible plants at one time in the same space, with each at different maturity level. Example: Intercrop two crops so one is growing beneath the shade or underlayer of a different, more mature crop. This creates a beneficial microclimate for the sheltered crop beneath.

Cut-and-come-again harvesting is a method of harvesting certain plants so they continue to grow even as you harvest some of their leaves. Harvest a few leaves but allow the growing point to remain intact and resprout. Then you can "come again" and harvest more leaves in a few weeks.

SAMPLE PLANTING PLAN

Start with a row of broccoli down the center of a raised bed as your Ace plant. They get the most space in the bed, and we want to protect and encourage them. Next, add in the Face cards: beets and onions. They're great companions, and we want an abundance of them. Encircle the broccoli with a mixture of beets and onions. Next, add some Plains, which will be the flowering herbs chamomile and sage. Then, to really put a chef's kiss on the design, add a nasturtium border in the front of the bed. It's a lower-lying plant, and you will still see the broccoli as it matures, along with the wisps of chamomile and onion tops.

This is the goal in the kitchen garden: layering plants that play nicely together as well as creating a stunning portrait in the landscape, and of course, feeding your family well.

Succession

The final step in the planning process is to consider what replaces this current round of plantings. For me, this includes what to grow in the next half season. For my Auntie Pammy (and perhaps you), this includes what to grow for the entire rest of the year. Each season has a few weeks of wiggle room that allow you to start early by either starting seeds inside, succession sowing, intercropping, or extending the growing season with tools like row covers and cold frames. Having a plan for what will immediately replace the crops you've already planned for or planted enables you to use your space most efficiently. For some plants, like corn, carrots, broccoli, cabbage, and anything that isn't cut-and-come-again, succession sow at least once to get two harvests a couple of weeks apart. For early planted cool-season crops like lettuce or peas, plan out what will replace them when the weather warms and they get pulled from the garden. Think about what will replace each crop as it is harvested to keep the kitchen garden moving and delivering as long as possible. You'll learn more about succession planting on page 72.

Rotation

There's an old expression when it comes to crop rotation: beans, roots, greens, fruits. This is a little rhyme to help you remember where to place your next set of vegetables as you're planning. Here is where the half season comes into play (or a full season if you're so lucky). This rhyme teaches us the order in which to best rotate the plants in each part of the garden. If you have beans in your raised bed in the spring and summer, then next you should plant a root crop (perhaps carrots) for the fall, and then the next crop to go into that bed the following spring is greens (maybe lettuce) and then after the lettuce is done, you plant something fruiting in its place, like a tomato or a

pepper. The science behind this is focused on the nutrients that each plant pulls from the ground. Beans are nitrogen fixers (meaning they take nitrogen from the air and convert it into a form that is used to fuel plant growth), so they are a great act to follow for the roots, which are gentle on the soil. Greens then come in and take some of the nitrogen now in the soil (their leaves love it), while leaving behind much of potassium that the fruiting crops that follow require. Then you can repeat the cycle and begin again with some type of beans. Voila!

Because of this, when it comes to planning, I like to think about the next set of plants to follow anything I've added to my planting map. This establishes a nice extra half-season plan in many cases. For example, after pulling garlic out in mid-summer, there is still time in our warm season for one more planting. Melons are a great replacement, as they like the late summer heat. With about seventy-five to ninety more days of garden goodness before pushing from warm to cool season, there is time for them to ripen.

As you can see by that example, crop rotation in the form of "beans, roots, greens, fruits" doesn't have to be a strict format you *must* follow. However, generally avoid sowing the same crops in the same place repeatedly as it will deplete your soil. Mix things up, even if it's only slightly, to keep the soil at its best.

▶ Peas are a crop that you sow once and harvest from all season to keep them producing.

The Kitchen Garden in Context

Another element that may nudge you to rotate crops is to think about proximity. Earlier, I mentioned a permaculture concept known as *rings of use* where the places and plants you need to access most frequently are placed in closer proximity to the home. Think about the entirety of your outdoor space and where the garden sits within that. The closest zone is right outside the door and therefore should hold the plants that you want the easiest and most frequent access to. This is typically herbs; however, as mentioned, I also mix herbs throughout the garden. I have a bed dedicated to herbs, which often grow perennially for me, *and* I have them in all the beds. The entire garden, depending on its size, may even fit into that first ring of use. Beyond that first zone, things are deprioritized as they are located further out in the garden. For my own garden, I have crops prioritized in order of use like this: herbs, leafy greens, seasonal crops like cucumber, tomato, and squash, then staple crops like potatoes and onions, then fruit and vines, and then the edible shrub and tree layer. Those distant zones are great for keeping pests and critters at bay. If we satiate things like birds, deer, and squirrels at a distance from where our own food source is, then we can naturally keep them in their own space and not in ours.

Your entire yard has the potential to be food-focused with edible landscaping and forageables. A kitchen garden is just one piece of the ecological puzzle. For this book, we'll stay focused on maximizing just our cultivated vegetable garden but reserve some space in your mind to think about which plants are most convenient to have close to you.

FOR THE LITTLE ONES

Each season I invite our children to choose some plants for the garden—both starts and seeds. With a little guidance, I let them choose what to grow and take full responsibility for their plants. One way to help this along is to give them their own plant stakes for marking the plants or to sow seeds in compostable pots so they can visually see and remember which plants are theirs. We started this tradition while at the plant nursery looking for starts to keep their hands full. They each got to choose a flower and carry it around with them, keeping their otherwise busy hands full with something precious of their own choosing. Now, the kids have so much enthusiasm for choosing their plants and know independently how to care for them.

QUICK GUIDE FOR GARDEN MAPPING

1. Make your plant list.
2. Decide on quantities.
3. Plan out what needs to be succession sowed or interplanted.
4. Place aces, then faces, then plains, then jokers.
5. Make sure to include a few herbs and flowers in each bed.
6. Use trellises and edges.
7. Plant closer together than you think.

◀ Mixing soil right outside the kitchen door by the potting bench makes for easy access when it comes to getting things done.

Trellis Building

An impactful part of any garden's design also lies in its structure. Even in a small home garden there is opportunity to build and layer. Trellises are key when it comes to saving space with vertical growing but also in creating a welcoming design.

Additionally, I find that there is no better work than that done by your own hands. My father used to call this "good old-fashioned hard work" and it is indeed satisfying. Though mostly an obedient child, I got a little riskier as a teenager and have one memory of being grounded. My family had purchased a porch swing from some big box retailer and thought it was a great opportunity to ground me for being out late. They made me build said swing as punishment, without the instruction manual. Once it was completed, I could resume my normal social schedule. They thought I'd be in for the weekend trying to figure it out, but I had that swing a-swingin' in less than two hours. Now I use the skill to configure a myriad of trellises in the garden and find that some of the most satisfying days of work are spent collecting sticks to teepee for my peas.

There are four go-to trellises I build time and time again with nothing but wood stakes and twine. They're easy and can be built as needed or beforehand. I get my stakes at the local nursery and prefer untreated redwood, as it's most rot resistant. Gathered sticks work too, as do fencing poles and t-posts. I find the most beautiful gardens often have a mix of materials and structures creating a lot of texture, layers, and perspectives. It's all quite beautifully personal, contributing to your story as a gardener and inspiring onlookers.

The truth about trellises is this: They're vitally important to the success of many plants. They allow the climbers and vining plants to do their work but also save space by encouraging vertical growth. Properly supporting plants is a key element in the kitchen garden and will vastly increase the footprint of your growing space.

FOUR GO-TO TRELLISES

Each of these trellises uses the same materials—6-foot (183-cm) untreated redwood stakes and jute twine. The redwood holds up well and the jute is durable, while also tightening with the dampness that is certain to occur in the morning dew. I keep these materials on hand, making my trellises quite modular, moveable, and personal to my needs for the season.

Pea Teepees

Pea teepees are a constant each year, though they often end up in a different place as I rotate crops. You simply use five or more stakes (I prefer seven) and make a teepee, driving one end of each stake into the ground at about a 45-degree angle, leaning the tops of the stakes in toward each other. I use jute twine to keep the top intact and then also to wind around and up the trellis, creating a spiral support for the peas as they climb. You can use this trellis for beans as well.

A teepee-style trellis.

An A-frame trellis.

The Florida weave trellis.

A-Frame Trellis

An A-frame trellis is fantastic for tomatoes, trellising them up with string that goes from the top of the frame into the ground, below the tomato plant. I like the vertical and horizontal support here.

Florida Weave

The Florida weave system is great for anything that bushes out, like fava beans or even tomatoes. It keeps plants upright and tightly woven between the strands of jute. Place your stakes in a row and then weave the jute around the stakes like layers of a basket, adding more layers of twine and increasing the height as the plants grow.

Box Trellis

A box trellis is more like a cage but much prettier. Place four stakes around your plant immediately after planting, then wind your jute around the box. This is fantastic for plants like pepper plants or tomatillos that need more horizontal support. These plants can technically grow without support, but they'll weaken as the fruit develops and the branches grow heavy. Providing a cage gives the fruit-laden stems a place to rest.

Adding personal touches into the garden with homemade trellises, plant tags, and even sculptures and other design elements is all a part of your garden's story. You can tell so much about a person just by looking at their garden. Allow yourself to play and get involved in building whatever

A box trellis.

you can—it's that "good old-fashioned hard work" that not only keeps you outside, but also keeps the garden productive.

A beautiful, bountiful garden is an evolving garden. It's moveable, personal, and some seasons, incredibly challenging. Once you have your garden set up it becomes a room just outside your home you get to adorn season after season to meet your needs—for food, joy, sanity, and fun. Some seasons feel heroic and like a masterpiece, and other seasons get gobbled up by the hectic pace of life or by Japanese beetles. But I assure you that with thoughtful plant placement, careful nurturing of your soil, and the consistent blessing of the garden with your own shadow, you will have a successful kitchen garden.

CHAPTER 3

GROW

The most foundational element in the garden—as obvious as it seems—is the soil. However, this part of the endeavor unfortunately leaves many people feeling overwhelmed, seeking advice from various sources, and often coming up with many confusing avenues to explore. What many gardeners are missing is the experience of a grandmother at our elbow, teaching us and proving to us that "dirt" will turn to soil with the right attention and care. We yearn for the wisdom of a storied guide, sharing their folklore as they fork in compost.

I have the privilege of a godmother who has been involved in my life since I was six weeks old. My Aunty Pammy, whom I first mentioned in the book's introduction, is calm, confident, and so very at ease with herself. Aunty Pammy always had a garden, and as I was growing up, I showed zero interest whatsoever in it or in her many other outdoor tasks. I was destined for the streets of New York City and never helped Aunty Pammy in her garden (or my parents' garden) a day in my life. That is, until I was thirty years old and started gardening myself. Aunty Pammy would call with tips for me. She never told me I was doing anything wrong; she would simply and gracefully suggest some approaches to try and share what she did with success in her space. A few years passed, and I had my third child. He was ten weeks old, and I was spending most days and nights balancing him wrapped to my chest with my other two kids

tugging at my hypothetical apron strings. It was spring, and Aunty Pammy came to my rescue and spent a weekend with us. For the first season in my life, I was honored to have her help me prepare my raised beds, teach me to can, and help me do *exactly* what she does—and has done for decades. And now I want to teach you.

I think it is also important to note the essential "living" component of this book's title. The living part of kitchen garden living is all about how the garden informs and enhances your life, how you fold it in, and how it inspires you to live purposefully. Everyone gardens differently, and the way you garden will inevitably become like a thumbprint for you—entirely unique. As we explore soil, seeds, sunlight, and so forth in the coming pages you may be tempted to think that there is a *best* way. There is no such thing. There is *your* way. If you get caught up thinking you need to start seeds indoors or get a greenhouse to have a successful garden, and yet the idea of all of that stresses you out or makes you feel paralyzed with indecision, then pause and think more simply—*What can I do now? How can I make this garden my own?* I'll share how I've done just that, and in doing so, created an odd and entirely unconventional approach I have yet to see anyone else do. Your garden will be entirely about your heart, needs, tastes, and climate, along with your house, your level of organization, and/or your desire to be unencumbered and free. Gardening is the ultimate experience of living true to you.

◄ As a child I thought I'd be walking on stages performing for a living, not walking through gardens teaching.

Soil

When it comes to the topic of soil, the first step is understanding the composition of your existing soil. This may be very poor form to share, but I've never lab-tested any of my soil. I just get in there with my hands and work in it. The professionals always soil test, though, and what such a test gives you are exact details on the macronutrients and micronutrients your soil either has or is lacking. As you mature and refine your gardening approach, testing may become ever more useful, or you may encounter a season where everything just dies. This is a great time to get a soil test and regroup by figuring out exactly which nutrients are needed.

We've had to overcome clay soil and soil full of cement and gravel, thanks to a botched renovation. We bought a house that was flipped and had a fabulous side yard for my garden. Frankly, the side yard was the only real reason I loved the house. It was a big, 500-square-foot (46.5-m²) patch of mulch, ready for raised beds. As we started to level the ground, we realized the construction crew had dumped spare pavers and the gravel roadbed (along with trash and plastic bottles!) there instead of paying to have it hauled to the dump. No doubt it saved them thousands of dollars, but we eventually had to pay for it as we remediated the site. Turning that "dirt" into soil would take years, so instead, we turned to raised beds to make our garden possible. There is an art and science to filling a raised bed, which we'll dig into in a later section.

THE IN-GROUND OPTION

For in-ground gardens, first determine your native soil type. It's smart to start out really getting to know your soil. The difference between dirt and soil? Dirt typically doesn't have nutrients in it. It can be barren and dry—basically like built-up dust. Soil, on the other hand, is alive, it's working, and there are organisms (some visible, some not) creating an ecosystem in which life is happening. The ideal soil composition for a healthy garden is just under half natural minerals (sand, silt, and clay

Adding fresh compost for the season and playing with worms.

particles), and then another half that is a mixture of air and water, with a small touch of organic matter from decomposed plant and animal matter. As we amend and build our soil over many years, we achieve this ideal composition, or at least encourage it to become as close as possible.

There are three main soil types:

1. Loamy soil is a perfect balance of *sticks-together-when-you-squeeze-it* and *not-too-hard-for-air-and-water-to-move-through*. This soil holds moisture but will crumble as well. It's a touch fluffy and smells clean.

2. Sandy soil is just that—sandy. It's very loose and drains quickly, making it hard for plants to uptake water because they can't access it. Sandy soil falls through your fingers easily without holding much shape.

3. Clay soil is very dense, and water has a hard time getting through, because it lacks air pockets. Much like artists' clay—when you hold it, it clumps together and dries out hard.

Whether your soil is clay-based or sandy, adding compost (organic matter) helps it retain water and creates proper aeration. All compost is not the same, so be aware of that and ask questions. If you're buying bagged compost, read the ingredients. You get what you pay for, so opt for certified organic composts if you can. Try to avoid composts with lots of ingredients (like a food label, less is more), and really try to see what the contents of the bag look and feel like. Many companies use fillers, like wood chips, in their bags, which is a sad shame. I have, however, found many reputable brands that are sold at nurseries; you just have to ask to see samples.

If you're buying bulk compost, seek out quality sources. Landscapers use bulk soil yards, some of which have compost mixes that are hot, meaning they are fresh, still decomposing, or not aged or turned. Call and ask questions about their compost and how it's made, describe your beds, and ask if the company has experience delivering to home gardens. You want bulk compost that is

Gardening in-ground with berms that we made on top of the soil to help break down our clay dirt.

In-Ground Bed Prep—No-Dig and One-Till

If you're gardening in-ground from scratch, your first step is to make your beds. There is something romantic about in-ground gardens. Our family did a one-month trip to Central Tennessee and all the home gardens were in-ground. Nary a raised bed in sight! If planting in-ground, I recommend a no-dig method, or a till-once method. This allows the good stuff (microorganisms, arthropods, fungal networks, etc.) to remain intact in the soil, and can help expand the garden's size slowly. There's a gardener in Britain, Charles Dowding, who is world-renowned for his no-dig methods.

The key to no-dig is to trust that the process works. All this garden-making business can be maddening, but no-dig is surprisingly easy! The premise is that even with existing grass or weeds, placing mulch on top of the ground eliminates light and smothers the grass or weeds while creating a natural and healthy area for you to create a garden. With no-dig, we are not in a rush for results and take our time to do things right. To create a no-dig garden, the first layer is a blocker such as cardboard or multiple layers of newspaper. They stifle anything below. Then add about 4 inches (10 cm) of compost and plant straight into that. Since the cardboard or newspaper layer decomposes after about three months, your plant's roots can go down into the native soil below. It truly is a simple approach.

One-till is another way to make new in-ground beds. It is a good method for areas that are mercilessly hard clay and have nothing growing there. With one-till, you skip the cardboard step and till the soil using a mechanical tiller or a shovel, if you prefer to do things by hand. Then layer the 4 inches (10 cm) of compost on top of the tilled bed. A little bit of gypsum under the compost helps break hardpacked clay down as well. And, while you certainly don't have to do this, you can also add temporary sides to your in-ground beds, maybe using old fence posts or 2 × 4s (5 × 10 cm), to keep the soil and new plants snug until the soil settles.

regularly aerated and aged, and no longer hot. The company can tell you if it can be used for food growing by home gardeners.

Don't create in-ground planting beds (or fill raised beds) with only compost—it's too light. Instead, *top* the beds with compost or mix some compost into the existing soil to create a loamy blend. I made the mistake one year of having too much compost, and water just drained through my beds. This was problematic as it increased the rate at which my beds would rot, and the plants couldn't uptake the water because it was slipping away.

The soil in in-ground gardens tends to be a bit trickier to control than raised beds, though they do leave you with many options. Amend an in-ground garden similarly to a raised bed, though I recommend adding more organic matter to in-ground gardens than I add to raised beds. For hard clay, gypsum can be a great option to add below your compost to break up compacted soil, with one single round of shallow tilling most-likely necessary. If your soil is sandy, you may not need to till at all, but instead add more compost into the mix to help sandy soils bind together, as well as some leaf mold or aged manure.

RAISED BEDS

Filling new raised beds can seem tricky, as there's much advice around the subject. I assure you most approaches will "work." Pick a path that matches the time, effort, and cost you want to put forth. This is the approach I take.

The anatomy of a raised bed starts with a base layer. Cardboard, sticks, dried leaves, and topsoil work well as the base layers. Once you get to the top 8 inches (20 cm), add more topsoil mixed with some coconut coir. Next, add 2 to 4 inches (5–10 cm) of finished compost, then a thin layer of worm castings, kelp meal, and crushed oyster shell. You can also calculate the proper amount of soil to fill the entire bed by using a cubic yards (or cubic meters) formula. This takes your raised bed depth, length, and width and gives you the amount of soil needed to fill each bed.

Here's how to calculate the soil volume needed to fill a bed:

First, multiply the length, width, and depth of your bed in feet to get the volume in cubic feet. To then get the equivalent measurement in cubic yards (which is what bulk soil is typically sold in), divide that number by twenty-seven to get the cubic yards. For example, if your raised beds are 8 feet long by 4 feet wide by 1.5 feet deep (2.4 × 1.2 × .5 m), your volume is 48 cubic feet (1.4 m³), or 1.8 cubic yards.

YEARLY SOIL PREP

Each season, no matter whether you grow in the ground or in raised beds, you'll amend your soil. Once each growing term has ended, we need to replenish nutrients. Even with perennials, it's good to side-dress seasonally.

Here's what I do to amend my 4- by 8-foot (1.2 × 2.4 m) raised beds:

- I add about 3 inches (7.5 cm) of compost to the entire bed. Seek out excellent compost and remember you get what you pay for when it comes to bagged products. Farm-sourced compost is even better.

NPK: WHAT DOES IT MEAN?

Nitrogen (N), phosphorus (P), and potassium (K) are the three primary essential nutrients required by plants, and most commercial fertilizers provide a combination of them in varying amounts, depending on the formulation. Often, gardeners don't need to fertilize at all, sometimes doing more harm than good by creating a dependency in our gardens and plants. However, with raised beds, it's hard to keep nutrition in and we're often moving plants in and out each season. When choosing a fertilizer, it's important to select one that is entirely organic, breaking down in a slow-release fashion so that it doesn't wastefully leech out of the soil. Later in the book we'll talk about homemade fertilizers made from plants, which is another great option.

- Next, I add about a ½ pound (225 g) of kelp meal to the bed, a bag of worm castings, and about a ½ pound (225 g) of crushed oyster shell or crushed crab shell. The shell is a source of calcium, which many fruiting plants like. I spread all the amendments in a thin layer and fork them into the top layer of the soil and compost. Then we're almost ready to go.
- Another final amendment I love to add as an alternative to fertilizer if I can are wool pellets. As they break down, they slow-release nitrogen into the soil, as well as help with aeration and pest control. There are tiny barbs in the wool that repel slugs and snails, keeping them away from the plants. It's a fantastic sustainable by-product recently being offered by small sheep farms.
- The final step, not to be forgotten: After you amend your garden (or fill your raised beds if they're new), soak the soil with water. Drench it so the water permeates through from the

Amend your soil each season with at least a mix of compost, kelp meal, worm castings, and calcium.

Starting Seeds

Ah, the most daunting part of the journey begins: seeds. They're so tiny and yet so complex, but don't be fooled by their hard exterior because they can also be easy. Take the time to play with seeds and surprise yourself. Children are the best helpers and can intuit where seeds need to go. We've had many a seed packet torn at the hands of a toddler only to find the plants grow fabulously even after being freed from the packet and stomped on, entirely by accident.

It's time to do some garden mathematics. As much as it pains me, I suggest doing the math stuff you're about to learn all at once and then note it in your garden journal for future years, so you don't have to do it again. To start your own seeds is to know your climate and your frost dates. If we're following the Northern Hemisphere's seasons, it is a great idea to cheat your spring season and start certain seeds indoors while there's still a chance of frost outdoors, especially if you live in a northern climate with a shorter growing season. You can then transplant those seedlings out into the garden at the first moment possible, as opposed to starting all seeds directly in the garden's ground where you'll miss about a month of growth that could have taken place inside. For autumn, there's a different set of seed-starting challenges, and for that season I recommend having a shade, water, and protection strategy for seeds being started mostly outdoors (more on this later). Regardless of whether you're planting seeds in the spring or in the fall, heat is the underlying theme, as seeds want a certain temperature for germination. All seeds also want near-constant moisture and as much light as a summer's day.

top down into the lower layers. I spend about 15 minutes per bed making sure the water is soaking down.

As you garden and prepare the soil, keep in mind the invisible science at play and working for your benefit. As you touch the soil and breathe it in, the tiny bacteria *Mycobacterium vaccae* (imperceptible microbes in the soil) are triggering the release of serotonin in your brain. Serotonin is a mood-booster hormone. It's as though the Earth knew we needed her—and not just at an arm's length, but to play and work with her intimately and often. The release of serotonin is a natural antidepressant, and it also enhances your immune system. Many studies have shown how gardening is directly tied to an increased quality of life.

For spring sowings of warm-season crops outdoors, begin with knowing your region's **last** expected frost date (a quick internet search of "last frost date" combined with your postal code will tell you). Then identify the amount of time it

▶ Filling seed trays with soil and vermiculite.

MY SEASONAL AMENDMENTS

- Compost
- Kelp meal
- Worm castings
- Crushed oyster shell or crab shell
- Wool pellets

Bottom watering seed trays is easy and effective.

takes for a particular seed to germinate. Subtract the number of days to germination from your last frost date and you have your first in-ground sow date. If you're starting these seeds indoors, tack on four to six weeks to that calculation. You do this because once seeds germinate, with their first two leaves, called *cotyledons*, coming up, we know the plant is prepared to mature. The next leaves to emerge are the first "true leaves." Ideally, each seedling has at least four true leaves before undergoing the process of hardening off, which is how plants are prepared for transplant outdoors (see sidebar, page 68). I like my seedlings to grow for about two weeks after those cotyledons come up to give them time to establish their true leaves before the hardening-off period.

For example:
- If your last expected frost date is April 15, and you're sowing cucumber seeds out into the garden that average seven days to germination, sow the seeds on April 8.
- If you're giving those same cucumber seeds a head start by growing them indoors first, take the last frost date of April 15, subtract the seven days to germination, and then subtract the additional four to six weeks for seedling growth. The ideal indoor planting date range would be between February 19 and March 10.

◄ Clociles are a great way to protect newly transplanted seedlings.

For fall sowings of cool-season crops outdoors, you'll do the same calculations, except use your **first** expected frost date (again, a quick internet search of "first frost date" and your postal code will tell you) and the number of days to maturity for that crop. Work backward from the first expected frost date by subtracting the number of days to maturity noted on the seed packet. That's the day to sow the seeds. Often seed starting outdoors is much easier in advance of the cool fall season, as the soil is still warm. The challenge here is that too much warmth can cause seedlings to prematurely bolt (go to flower and then to seed), and the heat will steal the soil moisture that you need for germination. Shade cloth on top of some hoops works wonders.

For example:
- If your first expected frost date is October 15, and you're sowing kale seeds, which average sixty days to maturity, sow the seeds out in the garden on August 15.

SEEDLING NEEDS

In general, seedlings need steady light from the sun or from grow lights, warmth via the sun or electric heat mats made specifically for seed starting, and a moist soil environment. Moist soil softens the seed coat and initiates germination. Watering daily is essential, and covering the seed tray with a sheet of plastic until the seeds germinate or regularly misting the top of the soil helps retain soil moisture. A thin layer of vermiculite on top of the soil is also very beneficial for helping the soil retain moisture with a lightness that won't disrupt the seed's germination.

For seed starting in trays or via soil blocking (see sidebar, page 70), the best seed-starting soil mix is a bit lighter and more porous than traditional garden soil. However, starting seeds in-ground out in the garden is, of course, good enough and wildly effective. Don't overthink it. However, making your seed-starting mix from scratch is a great way to increase the success rate.

A topping of vermiculite is a great way to keep soil moist when seed starting.

the seed-starting soil mix discussed in the last section, you'll also need grow lights to simulate sunlight if you don't have a bright window. Grow lights can be purchased online conveniently. The trick is to get the lights very close to the seed trays until the seeds germinate. After germination, adjust the lights to be slightly farther away—2 to 4 inches (5–10 cm) from the plant tops. You don't want the light too far away or the seedlings will get leggy. Adjusting lights on a pulley or having the ability to lower or raise your seed trays is helpful. Adding some tiny fans help with air flow and strengthen seedling stems that will eventually be exposed to the real wind. Waving your hand very gently through your seedlings once they have some true leaves achieves this as well.

In a pinch, I like to use traditional potting soil and add some coconut coir to make it even lighter. I avoid anything with peat moss in it as it is not only very slow to regenerate in bogs (think centuries), but when removed, it releases the carbon it had beautifully sequestered for tens of thousands of years. So, let's leave peat be. Coconut coir is a great option instead of peat moss.

Seed-Starting Soil Mix Recipe:

- 5 pounds (2268 g) organic raised bed soil
- 1 pound (455 g) compost
- 8 ounces (225 g) perlite
- ½ cup (68 g) blood meal
- ½ cup crushed oyster shells
- 8 ounces (227 g) coconut coir

SETTING UP AN INDOOR SEED-STARTING STATION

To create the ideal indoor seed-starting area, choose a cool, dry location with available electric. From the bottom up, you will need electric heat mats to create warmth for the seeds. Then you'll need seed-starting trays with drainage holes, as well as a flat tray without drainage holes below each to catch drainage water. In addition to

HARDENING OFF SEEDLINGS

Once your seedlings have their true leaves, if grown indoors, it's time to harden them off. Hardening off is the process of taking your plants outside incrementally into the true elements to help them adjust and strengthen gradually. This process should start about two weeks before your last expected frost date for warm-season crops, so the conditions aren't too harsh. Start hardening your plants off by putting them out in the sun for about an hour, then bring them back indoors. Increase the amount of time they are in the sun by an hour each day. Don't forget to bring them inside at night or they'll freeze. Set a timer on your phone and thank me later. I like to have all my seedlings on a tray, then place the tray on a table outside that is specifically for this task. I typically do this mid-morning as a starting point because the sun is the gentlest.

▶ Seed-starting soil ingredients with all the amendments, ready to mix.

One of my favorite techniques to avoid using those plastic cell trays for seed starting is soil blocking. Mix up a batch of seed-starting soil and get a large tray akin to one that you'd find in a cafeteria but with slightly taller sides. They sell such trays at nurseries and online. You'll also need a soil blocker, which is a fun tool you use to create little soil squares with a small dent in the top for seeds, hence the name *soil blocks*. This is the most cost effective and sustainable option for seed starting. Wet the soil so it is moist enough to stick together; a little moister than you'd typically have for seed starting in trays, but not runny. Then use the soil-blocking tool to push the soil together, packing it into the blocks tightly. Stamp the tool down and press the plunger, making perfect compact squares each with room for a seed. Fill your tray up with blocks and then sow your seeds. To water soil blocks, add water to the side of the tray, so the bottom of the blocks soaks up the water. Do not water from the top or the blocks will crumble.

The right moisture level is key for soil blocking.

If soil blocking doesn't feel approachable, using the more common seed trays is just fine. There are also bottom-watering trays. Some are even aluminum and can be reused for years. These are ideal as they result in strong and straight root systems since the roots reach down to soak up water.

The trick with indoor seed starting is to not forget to turn the lights on and off, as well as to adjust their height as your seedlings grow. Keep an eye on your seedlings and visit them once a day, adjusting things as necessary, running your hands over the sprouts to mimic the wind, and making sure moisture levels are adequate.

THINNING & POTTING UP SEEDLINGS

Once the seeds have germinated, it might be time to thin them. At the time of sowing, determine if you prefer to multi-sow, meaning you put more than one seed into each cell or block, or single sow, meaning only one seed goes into each cell or block. I multi-sow many types of seeds, knowing there will be a "spare" if one fails to germinate,

or I can thin them later if both do. To thin, once multiple plants have sprouted in the same cell, pinch or cut one of them. Avoid pulling out the extra seedlings; it can damage the fragile root growth of the remaining seedling. The stouter seedling is usually the healthiest, as opposed to the tallest sprout, which can be an indication of "legginess" and stretching for light. Simply snip off the cotyledons of those secondary sprouts and the seedling will soon die off.

The next step from here could be to pot-up your seedlings if they start to get big, but they aren't yet ready to plant out in the garden or the weather isn't cooperating. Plants left in their pots too long become root-bound, which means the roots get too big and start to grow around in a circle or otherwise get cramped. This can stress the plant or cause the soil to dry out more quickly.

A healthy seedling in a block of soil that is ready to be transplanted into the garden or potted up.

Starting seeds in the ground.

Up-potting (a.k.a. potting up) means carefully taking the entire seedling and its root mass and planting it into a larger pot. Be sure to use good potting soil and water the plants well, especially for the first few days after up-potting to make sure the plant doesn't undergo too much stress. Ideally, the less intervention the better. Keep in mind the size of the seed and plant and try starting larger plants in larger seed trays to avoid potting-up too many times or at all.

STARTING SEEDS OUTDOORS— A.K.A. DIRECT SOWING

If you are starting seeds outdoors, which I try to do as much as possible year-round, there are some things to note. Known as *direct sowing*, this method is the least amount of fuss. Simply use your last frost date to calculate the best time to start each type of seed and go from there (see page 67). If you have mulch in place, push it aside to sow seeds into the actual soil, only covering the soil around the seedlings back up with

PLANTS THAT PREFER TO BE DIRECT-SOWN

Seeds that prefer to be direct-sown are typically ones that don't like to have their roots disturbed. I've broken this rule and started these seeds indoors with success, but I do find some plants just like to set their roots in garden soil from the start and not be bothered with transplanting. Typically, root vegetables are best to sow right where you want them to grow, but a few other vegetables sit in this category too.

- Corn
- Beans
- Potatoes
- Onions
- Carrots
- Beets
- Sunflowers
- Peas
- Radish
- Turnips
- Parsnips
- Fava Beans
- Squash (winter and summer)
- Melons
- Cucumbers

A QUIRK OF MY GARDEN

One thing I discovered for my personal garden that I entirely adore is a tiny seed-starting greenhouse. You can also buy small full-sized greenhouses, but the one we use is a mini house (often called a *tabletop greenhouse*) covered with greenhouse-grade plastic and top panels that open and close. I place it on a raised bed or alongside the garden with seed-starting trays inside it. It gives me the ability to control my seed-starting climate, which needs to be warm on the tail end of our *cool* season and covered on the tail end of our *warm* season. The mini greenhouse has become a design element that is functional and makes seed starting something I look forward to, thanks to its cottage-core charm. It is a great example of finding unique solutions that work in your garden, adding some sweetness to your days and, of course, some protection to the plants.

The mini greenhouse in all its glory.

mulch after a few sets of true leaves form. The biggest challenge for direct-sown seeds is maintaining soil moisture, especially if you're planting in the warm season, and protection from pests. I highly recommend adding hoops and netting to any seed-sowing areas to avoid pests laying eggs on the tender seedlings. Young seedlings are perfect hosts for baby pests to be born onto and then munch away. Birds also love to eat seeds, and squirrels and rabbits love tiny sprouts. Don't say I didn't warn you. Have I cried at the sight of twenty Cheddar cauliflower seedlings being eaten down to stems one misty October morning? Yes, I have. Channel the potential future rage into the acquiring and installing of hoops and nets. The nets can also be interchanged for shade cloth when you start seeds in the warm season for fall harvests.

STAGGERED MATURITY DATES

As we do the dance of planning and planting the garden, there are benefits to planting crops with different maturity dates in the garden, which allows you to further maximize your yields from one crop. We discussed succession sowing in a previous chapter, but choosing varieties with differing maturation rates is another way to do this. Succession sowing is when you plant a set of plants or sow a set of seeds in succession every few weeks so that you have a continuous yield, which is great for plants that grow singularly, like carrots, beets, radishes, or broccoli. Once you harvest these plants, it's fantastic to have another set ready to harvest within a week or two so you can consume your seasonal ingredients in real time, as opposed to having everything ready at once, pushing you into preservation-mode.

Having staggered maturity rates is an additional hack. This involves planting different varieties of each plant, each of which matures at a different time. Beets are a great example. The varieties Touchstone Gold and Detroit Red mature at different rates. Touchstone Gold matures in 55 days, while Detroit Red matures in 95 days. This creates a natural succession rate for harvest, so even if you sow them both on the same day, you'll have intermittent beets available. Using succession sowing and staggered maturity dates is kitchen gardening at its finest—planning for continuity within your growing season and maximizing your nutritional uptake, while getting to enjoy the many varieties of a single plant.

Watering and Irrigation

Another crucial aspect of gardening is having a watering plan. As I mentioned previously, I dragged a 100-foot (30.5-m)-long hose through our townhouse to water my first garden. First, our hose bib was in the back of the house, and our garden was in the front. Second, I told our homeowners association I would cover the cost of water as a part of my plan to get to use community land for the garden. It was no big deal, and it created a wonderful habit of checking the garden daily. Watering by hand is acceptable, cheap, and easy. I was intimidated by automatic irrigation in the beginning, avoiding it entirely by choice.

Adjusting my soaker hoses that are hooked up to hose bibs in each raised bed.

If you have a larger garden, want more freedom, or like the idea of automating a task, then timed automatic irrigation is the way to go. Most commonly people use an available hose bib and attach irrigation tubing to it, with emitters coming off the tubing, or via attachments placed near each plant. I use soaker hoses because I love how they can be moved around very flexibly. They need to be replaced every few years, but it's not a difficult endeavor. We discussed already how having irrigation pipes dug into trenches below ground is ideal to save you from having unsightly tubing all over the place, but it's not essential. If you do have buried irrigation pipes, there will likely be PVC piping extending up into each individual bed—ideally against an edge—with a valve attachment that some type of irrigation, such as soaker hose or sprinkler emitters, can be attached to. This is the most flexible and efficient method of designing and setting up the garden's water supply for the long term.

Overhead sprinklers are an option too. I know many cut-flower farmers who use this method. However, I don't recommend it for all climates. The petals and leaves of the plants aren't what need the water; the roots are. Watering at the base of your plants to target the root zone is most effective.

Your life's rhythm will dictate how watering goes. This is why hand-watering comes highly recommended and is almost a gift to you as the gardener. It's a moving meditation; it gets you out there. It can be hard to understand how much water the garden is getting, though, and you are likely to water less than you should. Keep this in mind. To check the moisture level, simply stick your finger into the soil, up past your knuckles. Pull your finger out and if there's soil stuck to it, you're good. The soil is damp enough. If your finger is dry, you need to water. You will need to adjust water based on the weather, of course, making summer most taxing on the plants.

It's best to water the garden when the water can be retained and given time to travel up the plant's roots. Early morning is a great idea in most seasons. After dusk can be a great time as well, ensuring the heat of the day has passed, though the soil does hold on to some of that warmth.

All the details of getting your garden going and growing can feel insurmountable when reading about them all at once. Of course, you could just pull on some boots, fill your hands with seeds, and haphazardly start plopping them in the ground. Give them a glug of water, return to your life, and things will happen. It can be that easy. Keep the basics in mind: good soil, water, heat, and sun. Building your instincts up around this is as important as the task itself. The beauty in the journey of doing all the things draws you nearer and nearer to nature and to yourself. Get to know the language of soil dampness and seed sprouts. It's enchanting. Awe-inspiring and always different, your garden is now your teacher.

FOR THE LITTLE ONES

Children are so happy to help with garden setup and turnover each season because there's not much they can mess up. Let them rake in soil amendments, water down beds, dump out worm castings, dig furrows for seeds, help pin down irrigation, place plant markers, sow seeds, and collect leaves for mulch or bed-filling. We typically task the willing kids with finding any grubs to remove from the garden as we turn our beds, as well as evening out soil and collecting and throwing away any loose bags or debris.

▶ How you get gardening done with little ones—include them!

CHAPTER 4

TEND

I am at odds with the "tending" message I want to share with the world, as I truly and deeply believe we need to be outside and in the garden as much as we can. Nature heals you, makes you better, calms your nervous system, clears your mind, hugs your anxiety, and reduces your depression. You *can* get away with only about ten minutes a day in your garden should you happen to be in a busy season (a.k.a. an "exhale" season of life). That being said, I enjoy few things as much as all the tending and prefer to spend far more time than that in the garden when I can. It's like being able to dote on your children without onlookers thinking you're spoiling them, while also giving a feeling of renewal akin to moving the couch in the living room. There's much to be done in the garden, and good reason for it.

Most of the tending done mid-season helps plants stay strong, resist pests and disease, and continue to produce at a higher level than if you opted out of some tasks. Some edible plants are "set it and forget it," but it depends on your climate and the health of your soil. Strong soil creates resilient plants. My pumpkins are typically something I literally do nothing with. I let them sprawl out and get wild and crazy, and they just produce like nobody's business. Near the end of the season, if they're encroaching on other parts of the garden, I'll prune a bit, but that's it. Other plants require a lot more maintenance.

So, what is there to do? Let's break it down based on the elements: sun, soil, air, water, and growth (a bonus category!).

◄ There's an art to finding the perfect balance in tending to your garden while also letting it reach the potential that nature intended.

Sun:
Shade and Trellises

When the sun is one of your top challenges (either too much or not enough), there are a few solutions to employ in the beginning or middle of any season. You can create shade based on how the garden is mapped out, which I mentioned in chapter 2, with the placement of tall plants, as well as by utilizing intercropping as a planting method that can increase or decrease available sunlight.

To *maximize* your sun exposure, use trellises. They get vining plants up off the ground. Trellising plants also creates fantastic and necessary airflow. However, if you need to *minimize* your sun exposure, which is a big concern during the mid- to late-warm season, you'll want some shade-creation ideas. A great DIY is to get hoops for the garden. They're typically wire or plastic rods that are bent

A pea teepee can provide great shade for crops that need a reprieve from the harsh afternoon sun.

in a half-circle shape and placed into the soil in a row so shade cloth can be draped over them (or garden fleece for winter). Hoop covers are also a fantastic solution for any plants being attacked by bugs. They are particularly useful for covering seeds you're trying to germinate and keep moist for a late warm-season sowing. I have a few sets of wire hoops and shade cloth I put out each summer and fall. I also love to use hedge trimmings of long pliable branches to create beautiful, foraged hoops. As they dry out, they harden and become the perfect natural solution.

Soil:
Amending,
Side-Dressing,
and Weeding

Keeping the soil dialed-in is really where the gardener should be most particular. The start of each season is the best opportunity for improving the soil. However, there are a few things to do throughout the season to keep your soil full of nutrients to support your plants. If you're growing leafy greens, a great mid-season additive is a nitrogen-supplying fertilizer. Bloodmeal is great for this. Comfrey is another option. Chop some comfrey leaves down and use them as a mulch or top dressing. They'll eventually decompose into the soil. Comfrey tea, which is aerated and used as a fertilizer (explained on page 123 in detail), is another possibility. It's all natural and a great boost for your soil. It not only provides nitrogen, but also potassium, which helps with a range of other flower- and fruit-producing plants.

Adding fertilizers after plants are already tucked into their beds is called *side-dressing*. To top dress, sprinkle (or pour, if it's a liquid product) the material on top of the soil, about 2 to 3 inches (5–7.5 cm) away from the stems of the plants,

Carrying a batch of comfrey tea out before naptime for the baby.

Staking some eggplant with half a bamboo stake.

and then lightly scratch it into the soil's surface. I recommend you do this at dusk, after the heat of the day, to avoid burning any leaves or roots. Be gentle and disturb the soil as little as possible. This is great to do with liquid fish emulsion or liquid seaweed, both of which add a boost of nutrients, or the comfrey fertilizer.

Finally, it's time to discuss the task we most associate with childhood chores: weeding. Every time I weed, I'm reminded of how we also should be weeding our minds and our lives. The task is meditative, simple, and space-making. It allows the good stuff to grow, makes room to plant more, and showcases the garden's future potential once completed. Weeding our minds—perhaps even as we weed the garden—culls negative thoughts and replaces them with affirmations or mantras. Weeding our lives means distancing ourselves from people who don't contribute positively to our lives. It means changing behaviors that don't serve us and replacing them with healthy habits.

Much like thoughts and feelings, what makes a weed a weed is entirely subjective. Dandelions have beautiful medicinal powers and wish-making magic. Clover can be made into a nurturing tea, and stinging nettle has hundreds of beneficial uses. All three are classified in modern times as weeds. Thousands of additional "weeds" are edible and useful; they may just be growing where they aren't wanted. Even the most stunning rose could be considered a weed if it's growing in the wrong place.

My recommendation for weeding is to do it by hand, never with toxic or synthetic chemical applications. Burning out weeds with a propane torch, especially if they are coming up between gravel or pavers, is an option, too. If you find weeds are taking over a space, think about what you can do to occupy the space with something useful instead. A full vegetable garden has very little space for unwanted things, which is why interplanting beds more lushly than a conventional seed packet would advise prevents weeds. I take this approach with my kids—if they have time to act out, they have time to be helpful. I've found my wildest child has very useful energy and enthusiasm when directed toward tasks like helping me cook or garden.

Air:
Pruning and Staking

Increasing airflow in the garden discourages the spread of disease and fungus. It also prevents certain pests from accumulating. Aphids love to congregate! Pruning plants throughout the growing season is a great way to keep things moving and thriving. For pruning in the vegetable patch, here are some plant-specific approaches:

- For squash or zucchini, prune away yellowing or mildewed leaves. This applies to cucumbers and leafy greens as well. Be careful not to prune too much, as the plant needs leaves to soak up the sun and feed itself.
- For tomatoes, trellis them up a string or a pole or cage, and prune them a lot and early on. Once there is some healthy growth— at least six sets of true leaves—prune the suckers off (the small stems growing in the 45-degree angle between the main stem and a leaf offshoot), as well as the bottom set of leaves. This encourages the plant to produce more fruit and stronger roots, as well as creates good airflow.

For staking tasks, focus on bushy varieties, like bush beans, tomatillos, peppers, determinate tomatoes, yarrow, fava beans, dahlias, or any other plants with the potential to become heavy-sided or that produce heavy blooms. If you don't add support, they flop over or the stems break. To stake plants, simply use a tall piece of wood (bamboo or redwood stakes work—or even random branches about ½-inch (1-cm) thick) and push it into the soil 2 inches (5 cm) from the plant's base (to give the roots some room). Use twine, Velcro strips, or twist ties to fasten the main stem to the stake loosely. I love the way this makes the garden look, giving some formality to the wild plants that do better when they're supported.

It is wise to place your stakes at the time of seeding or planting, as opposed to inserting them

Peppers love to be tended to with pinching when they're young, staking as they age, and some fish fertilizer while they grow.

after the plants have grown unruly. The process is like trellising, but it requires a bit more guidance from the gardener as the plant grows. Staking is something I am always tinkering around with, especially during my morning walks in the garden.

Water:
Providing Enough

While we discussed watering and irrigation at the end of the previous chapter, there is more to say about the matter, and it has to do with timing and retention.

The best time of day for watering is very early morning. The next best time is just before or after dusk. The water needs to be able to soak down deeply into the soil, allowing roots to easily uptake it. Watering midday results in too much evaporation, losing much of the water before the plants get a drink. As your growing season gets cooler toward its end, don't water during the coldest part of the night.

▶ Bushy plants like peppers and tomatoes need to be staked.

Water retention in the soil is important for supporting the roots and ensuring the plant can draw in certain nutrients. It's especially critical for germinating seeds. They need continual moisture to sprout. My two favorite ways to keep water in the soil are with mulch or with vermiculite. Use mulch in your garden beds year-round to hold in soil moisture. Shredded leaves and straw are good options for vegetable gardens. Densely planted vegetable beds may not need mulch because the plants help shade the soil and prevent water loss. When growing seeds, vermiculite is another option. Use it as a topping for seeds you're waiting to germinate. Cover the soil with a gentle sprinkling to hold moisture in.

Growth: So Many Tasks!

An analogy I often can't stop thinking about as I garden is this: The more you harvest, the more you get. Also: The more you weed, the more you come to realize how many weeds there are. And doesn't it always feel like the more work you do, the more work you see? All of this is to say, it's not until you're working in the trenches that you see the potential. Whether we're talking about the garden or life in general, harvest the good stuff, weed out the bad, and don't be afraid of a little hard work because it helps you see all the possibilities ahead. In the garden, pinching and harvesting are two chores that play into this. For many plants, the more frequently you harvest from them, the more flowers and fruits they produce. The practice of pinching is also all about increasing a plant's potential. When you pinch certain plants, you increase the number of blooms they produce and help manage their growth. Let's talk about both tending practices next.

This tomato seedling is the perfect size to pinch, creating a two-leader system and a plant with twice the fruit.

PINCHING

There are many plants that benefit greatly from regular pinching. Pinching is the act of cutting or pinching off some of the buds or shoots. Sometimes this is to tell the plant to push down stronger roots before it flowers. Other times it's to force it to grow more side-shoots, which creates more flowers or stems for fruit. Tomatoes, for example, can be pinched, which turns a vine with one branch into a vine with two, which means there's twice the potential for fruit! This is called a *two-leader system*. Peppers and snapdragons can also be pinched: Cut off the first stem shoot at its tip and then the plant produces two side shoots with taller and stronger stems and blossoms. This feels cruel and counter-intuitive to some gardeners, but I assure you it's helpful. It is, however, optional. Play with pinching in your garden and see what feels good for you.

If you harvest tomatoes just as they start to blush, they can finish ripening inside on the counter.

PLANTS TO PINCH

- Snapdragons
- Tomatoes
- Peppers
- Basil
- Dahlias
- Marigolds
- Geraniums
- Sweet peas

HARVESTING

Oh, how I love that some plants love to give and give! Herbs, flowers, indeterminate tomatoes, beans, and cucumbers provide such an abundance. In fact, with beans and cucumbers, if you don't harvest them regularly, the plant stops producing and pushes toward seed production faster. If you're growing dry beans and seed production is the point, then don't harvest them green. Let them dry on the vine so you can collect them for your pantry. But if you're enjoying fresh produce, harvest as often as you can so the plant uses its energy to create even more harvests for you.

There are also cut-and-come-again plants, including herbs, lettuces, greens, green onions, chives, and others. To harvest in this style, only pick a few outer leaves but leave the growing point—you'll be able to return to the plant repeatedly to harvest more. Cut-and-come-again plants continue producing leaves from the center growing point of the plant, so always harvest from the outer portion. This is what makes a lettuce patch live for months and months—take a little from each plant and allow it to keep growing. Same goes for leafy herbs like basil and parsley. Get out there and use them! They'll keep producing foliage, and consistently harvesting it keeps them from going to flower, at which point they become bitter.

The garden becomes like your partner in a dance as you develop a rhythm and get to know each plant and the care it needs. The first year or two may feel heavy, but once you develop some intuition around it, a mere ten minutes a day tending your garden works wonders. I often go out in the morning to survey the landscape and take mental notes, pinching and pruning by hand for a few minutes and then return to harvest for dinner around dusk. There is only one perfect way to do this, and that way is *your* way.

TENDING TOOLS FOR THE KITCHEN GARDEN

I believe it was Martha Stewart, the domestic and garden goddess that she is, who told us you must use the right tool for the right job. She's not wrong; however, I'm a "less is more" kind of gal, so just the essentials have worked fine for me.

The kitchen garden is unique in that it's a smaller scale typically. We may not need a broad fork and we don't need a tiller. However, there are a few tools I always have on hand.

1. **Good clippers/shears** are of course what we need for harvesting, pinching, and pruning. Keep them clean and sharp and try to keep them out of the rain. I also use scissors from time to time, but a great pair of clippers is worth it. I do prefer having three types. One long-handled hedge trimmer for doing exactly that and for pruning roses (they let you keep a distance from the thorns), trimming tall or climbing plants, and for cutting pretty blooming branches while foraging. I also like to have a traditional garden pruner that fits comfortably in your hand and has half-moon bypass blades. Lastly, some little snippers for herbs and quick little in-and-out tasks are nice to have as well. These are always in my pocket.

Some favorite gardening tools, including the ever-so-useful ice scoop.

2. **Twine** is such an underrated workhorse in my house and garden. It gives such a fun touch of nostalgia and rustic charm to gifts and harvest bundles for sharing. Twine is also the queen of my homemade trellises (jute specifically because it tightens when wet). In addition, I use it for plant staking and tying up herbs for drying. It's indispensable, and I often buy it in bulk or in the checkout line at the craft store.

3. Here's a fun one: an **ice scooper**! I love the size of a metal ice scoop for scooping soil. It holds four times the volume of a garden trowel and fills seed trays in half the time. I also use it for scooping out worm castings, wool pellets, and other scoopable stuff.

4. A **dibber** is a sweet little tool to measure depth when planting seeds or bulbs. I love to eyeball measurements, but many seeds have a required planting depth if you want them to have good germination rates. Bulbs like a certain sweet spot when it comes to planting depth, so using a dibbler keeps it consistent.

5. Often sold as a pair, a **trowel and hand fork** are garden classics for a reason. They're the most-used tools because they do what we need: Spread and dig. Even the most feral of gardeners will enjoy these conveniences. I like a basic trowel, but a small spade with a serrated edge is handy for digging into compacted soil.

6. **Hoops** will save you. I've extolled their benefits in earlier sections, but I'm going to do it again. Invest in them. They are great for supporting shade cloth at the height of summer, frost cloth in winter, and netting protection from birds and critters throughout the growing season. Trust me on this: You want these. Buy a set that's the exact size you need or build your own with PVC pipe. Some companies make them in adjustable forms so you can change the size/height as needed.

7. My final favorite tool to always have on hand are **plant tags**. There was a time when I never had these when I needed them. There were many urgent moments before a rain came when I needed to seed radishes or some other plant but didn't want to forget where I'd planted them. In those moments, I could never find my plant tags. Now, I keep a stock of plant tags with a permanent marker hidden somewhere nearby (but not where the rest of the family will accidentally find them!).

PERMACULTURE AT HOME

As we learn more about the benefits of biodiversity, it becomes evident that the ultimate control of the gardener is not only a fallacy, but also counterproductive to the long-term health of our gardens and the overall environment. Permaculture, by definition, is the practice of creating self-sufficient and sustainable systems of agriculture, of which our kitchen gardens are a part. This shift from imposing our will at whatever cost to gently tending in a way that is inclusive of insects good and bad, critters, and even the whole of nature is indeed a new way of trying to manage a garden to produce food for the home.

The goal now becomes to tend much less and instead plant in a way that reduces the need for human intervention and management. That being said, I believe a gardener's shadow is the best fertilizer. Our presence in moving things about, helping nudge soil along, and trying to interpret clues from nature to inform our decisions are great ways to think about our role as gardeners, rather than demanding or expecting ultimate control.

A gardener's shadow really is the best fertilizer.

DIVIDING PLANTS

One tending task in the garden that feels frightening and always makes me wonder, "Am I doing this right?" is dividing perennial plants. With all the fussing we do over root systems and keeping plants alive, it's amazing to see how resilient they are. In the kitchen garden, I can't stress enough the importance of including perennial plants. They're the backbone of pollinator support, and they provide a mature character to outdoor spaces. They're wildly important for creating biodiversity, drawing in pollinators like native bees and butterflies, and keeping negative pests at bay. I also love certain perennials for the "landscaped look" they provide while also being edible. Lemongrass is one such staple, as is salvia, sage, coneflower, rose, bay laurel, pineapple guava, dogwood, and many other varieties of flowering perennials, depending on your growing zone and region.

Many perennials can be divided and replanted in the garden (or shared with a friend), and the process is easier than you think. Gently dig up the plant, making sure to remove the entire root ball. It should give way to your shovel and come up in one big heave. Then, do a mixture of pulling at the base of the plant with one hand while putting pressure on the root ball with the other to create some seams in the root ball, resulting in small, easy-to-pull-apart root sections. Other, thicker-rooted perennials may need to have their clumps divided into smaller sections with a good chop of a sharp shovel. You can then take your now-separated plants and place them elsewhere in the garden, filling out borders and making an even lusher landscape.

▶ Harvest your garden regularly to keep plants producing. I like to harvest in the cool of the morning.

PLANTS THAT SHOULD BE REGULARLY DIVIDED

- Coneflower (Echinacea)
- Lemongrass
- Peony
- Iris
- Yarrow
- Rudbeckia
- Hosta
- Phlox
- Delphinium
- Dianthus

A late summer crop of lettuce is planted in the shade of the corn stalks.

INTERPLANTING FOR PROTECTION

One brilliant garden "hack," if you will, is learning how to cheat the seasons. As you already know, interplanting is just the ticket for maximizing your space, but it also enables you to protect certain plants and grow them during a time when they won't usually grow. Weaving plants together that may otherwise not do well in a particular season can afford them some protection. For instance, lettuce and spinach have a hard time in the heat. However, if they are interplanted with something that casts a thick shade, it keeps them cool. Once the garden is really moving in the warm season, perhaps there are a few feet of tall corn plants in a row or beans climbing a trellis, casting a great chunk of shade. That's the place to plant spinach or lettuce. Both are fast to grow, shallow-rooted, and enjoy the cool reprieve from direct sun. This is a great way to also add in plants mid-season or sow some last-minute seeds if there is some empty space in the garden. Do a little research on a spinach or lettuce variety that is heat tolerant and "slow to bolt." Some of my favorites are Butterhead lettuce and Olympia spinach.

To successfully interplant in this way, refer to the notes on companion planting (see page 45) to be sure everything complements each other well. Note the root depth of each plant so there is not a tangle of competing roots underground. Plant shallow-rooted crops amongst deep-root vegetables that produce edible leaves or fruit. And of course, don't overlook tucking in herbs and flowers. Pansies and violas, for example, can be grown almost year-round in our climate if they are properly shaded during summer's heat.

It's all about timing. Sneaking a crop into the garden mid-season, or banking on a slow-to-mature variety taking its time while the plants it's interplanted with grow much faster, is a wonderful way to get more out of your kitchen garden.

◀ Dahlias famously love to have their tubers divided at the end of the season, allowing you to have even more blooms the following year for free.

SEASON EXTENDING

Season extension is another garden-tending trick to keep in your back pocket. As I've mentioned before, at the beginning of the growing season, most gardeners want to start early to get a jump on planting. These folks start their seeds indoors for this reason, and the moment the danger of frost has passed, the seedlings go into the garden. Later in the season, we're often trying to get plants that prefer cooler temps into the ground as the heat is waning, but not gone. We've discussed this when it comes to seed starting, but I want to further stress this strategy to you.

To help maximize the kitchen garden's lifecycle, let's explore how to extend the seasons so you can grow as close to year-round as possible. As I just mentioned, to get a jump on the warm season, starting seeds indoors is the way to go. And then on the back end of the warm season is the seam between that hot weather and the coming cool season. Once again, this is where hoops and shade cloth are masterful and open the garden to new plants while you're still reaping the benefits of the current season. Typically, by the end of summer in the Northern Hemisphere, tomatoes are still going crazy, the eggplants are finally coming to the party, and the peppers won't quit producing. It's lovely, but we also want to make sure we have enough time to sneak in a round of cool-weather-loving brassicas for fall harvesting. It's a tricky balance, and many people ask me when I know it's time to pull out the summer crops and make way for the next wave. It's a personal preference, of course, but try to time things so the very first round of cool-season crops goes in about one to two months before the sunlight starts to fade at the beginning of autumn.

The hoops and shade cloth protect new plant babies from the harsh end-of-season sun, which is great for germinating seeds but not-so-great after they sprout. Additionally, the end of the hot season often brings out a lot of pests. A second generation of many pest insects is in the larvae stage. These larvae either eat the roots or shoots

Placing hoops for shade cloth to extend the season.

of plants, depending on the species. A great pest strategy is essential during those swing seasons.

COMMON PESTS

Some common pests encountered in my garden near the stressed end of a season are rats and squirrels, Japanese beetles, grasshoppers, vine borers, and hornworms. Earlier in the warm season it's caterpillars and aphids, while during the late season when temperatures are cooler, the trouble comes from grubs that stay warm underground as they grow. What pests you face in your garden will likely be different because all zones and gardens encounter different things.

A few pest management quick tips:

- Before placing and filling new raised garden beds, install gopher wire (a.k.a. metal hardware cloth) in the bottom so they can't dig up into your beds from the base. Don't skip this step. Beg, borrow, or steal if you must. Caging gardens in general is the best way to keep out critters. For us, ground squirrels are a particular breed of hellion that cannot be deterred except with fencing. Later in the book I share my peppermint diffuser instructions, which I have found useful to keep rats away.

- With grubs, the only effective method for us is hand removal (bribe the children if you must) combined with a generous application of beneficial nematodes to the soil.
- For beetles and hornworms, a useful trick is to cover the fruit or veggies being attacked with little organza or gauze bags (like the ones you'd find a bracelet sold in). The sun can get through the bags, they're easy to put on and off, and they keep insects at bay.

Nurseries also sell some amazing hi-tech pest control options that emit sounds, spray water, or otherwise scare pests away. These are a good investment.

Take comfort in knowing this: All gardeners need to manage pests from time to time. In an organic garden, pests are par for the course. It's more about maintaining a balance. Learn to accept that some crops will never leave the garden due to pest damage, but there will still be plenty that does make its way to the kitchen. Plant accordingly.

Seed Saving

Saving seeds seemed silly to me once upon a time. I felt seeds were so abundant and easily available and collecting them myself was sort of a banal task. However, now that I'm slipping into the age of "I remember when" and I've lived through quite a few atrocities that have proven how our reliance on outside sources is a great way to create anxiety and dependence, I feel differently. It might seem dramatic, but simple acts like seed saving build inner strength, confidence, and of course, resourcefulness. Additionally, saving seeds

from plants that were successful in your garden means the next generation of that plant is better adapted and better suited to your unique garden conditions. How fantastic and magical is that? The plant adapts to survive and best live where it's rooted, so in turn, it puts out seeds that will do the same. Genius.

The first event that really shook me regarding food security and seed access was the COVID-19 pandemic. In 2020 there was a perceived seed shortage as millions of new gardeners hit the scene, panicking from a failed trip to the grocery store where shelves were empty, while also being stuck inside under quarantine. It was a bit of a wakeup call for so many new and experienced gardeners alike, helping us all see how fragile our food system is. This is when seed saving became important to me and many other gardeners. Additionally, many seeds in this modern century have been hybridized, some to create better results for the home gardener and some so big farms can grow crops that are more uniform. Some commercial crops have also been genetically modified, which is a whole different issue. Saving my own organic, open-pollinated heirloom seeds is what I'm after these days, hoping to be a part of saving excellent seeds to be passed on for future generations.

The kids harvesting cosmos seeds to save for planting next year.

Harvesting scarlet runner beans for saving so they can be replanted next season.

The key to saving seeds lies in letting the plants you want to collect seed from die back all the way and fully complete their life cycle. It's wildly satisfying to see this happen and feel the seeds just gently glide into your hands when they are ready for collection. Cosmos always shed their seeds so gracefully, which may explain why they are so prolific to the point of being obnoxious spreaders in my garden. Some seeds, however, are encased in a pod or hidden inside the vegetable or fruit, making them a bit more challenging to collect.

To save seeds inside of a fruit or vegetable, collect the very ripe fruits, squeeze or scoop out the seeds, rinse them clean, and dry them. Even tomato seeds are easily saved if you shake them into a glass of water, stir briskly to remove the "goop," strain off the water, and then let them dry. Let the seeds sit, spread out on a coffee filter, in a cool place with some airflow, making sure nothing molds.

For seeds in a pod, like beans or peas, leave some of the ripened pods on the vine until they fully dry out and turn into a papery, yellow, or brown husk, and the beans or peas inside harden. Harvest the seeds and let them further dry indoors.

I always think of the quote, "Cut your own firewood and it will warm you twice" when planning for seed saving. If you're going to save seeds, plant extra plants. You're growing some for now and some for the future.

Here are some tips for storing your saved seeds:
- Paper envelopes with written labels are great for storing each seed type separately.
- Note the date the seeds were collected, the variety, and the color, if needed.
- Organize your seed envelopes by season and sow-date.
- Be sure the seeds are completely dry before storing.
- Keep packed seeds in a cool, dry place.

Seed gathering is typically an autumn task: a time when gardeners are often looking for ways to connect to nature before winter settles in. I quickly fill labeled glass jars with collected seeds and then shuffle them into a more permanent storage situation as the season shifts and winter gives me more time to tackle the project properly.

The final step in saving seeds is organizing them. This is an ongoing feat with many possible options. One way to organize and store seeds is to use a large photo-organizing bin. These plastic cases have a bunch of smaller 4 × 6-inch (10 × 15-cm) cases within them, each perfectly sized for seed packets. I categorize my seeds by type and season. I have some spring- and fall-sown seeds together in cases and then I have other cases for larger groups like tomatoes, herbs, wildflowers, peas, and so on. Another method is to use a three-ring binder with clear photo album display pages inside. Instead of holding photos, each page holds seed packets. Pages with four inserts each are most common. This method is great for visual gardeners.

No matter how they are organized, keep your seeds in a cool, dark, dry place so they last as long as possible. The typical lifespan of a seed depends on its variety, but seeds can remain viable far beyond their expected lifespan if they are properly stored.

Keeping a Garden Journal

The capstone on setting up your garden is getting and maintaining a garden journal. Journals are a personal record of what's happening in the garden, how well plants are doing, where you placed them, what pests came around, what's being harvested, and any other items you want to track. Each season it's nice to go back to the year prior and review what did well, when you sowed things, what the weather was like, and your germination rate.

Every season I hand-draw my beds in my journal, sketching what goes where, and moving things about as needed. It's the creative download I need to keep the garden in order and to visualize the space properly. I love to use a notebook with gridded pages and just freeform all the info. I have many friends who have journals passed down from their mother or grandmother, and I can think of few greater treasures and comforts to pass down to the next generation. While I'm not always vigilant in my garden journaling, I do think it's a nonnegotiable part of the endeavor.

Here are some specifics to keep track of for each growing season:

- The season and year
- The specific variety of each plant in the garden
- How many plants you've planted
- Whether it was planted as a seed or a start
- Date of planting, sowing, or transplanting
- Companion plants used
- Soil amendments used (if applicable)
- Pest or disease issues
- Any prevention or treatment for pests or diseases
- Harvest dates
- Harvest quantities

FOR THE LITTLE ONES

I have a rubber stamp that has a cute design on it and a place to fill in "seed type" and "date collected" for my paper seed-saving envelopes. This is the perfect task for children, as stamping is one of life's most satisfying efforts when you're little. Depending on the seed, I'll have the kids help gather them and lay them out to dry, and then stamp the envelopes. As they get older, let them count out however many seeds per envelope you'd like.

Sketching your beds out in a journal each season keeps things creative, well-rotated, and organized.

Planting pink Chinese celery into a pot.

Not to completely disillusion you, but I rarely take the time to jot down all this info into my own garden journal, mainly because, at the time of this book's writing and publication, I have three children under the age of six, and I feel lucky just to get a moment to sow a seed. I'll never forget how a couple of autumns ago, my son ripped a packet of bok choi seeds open, dumped it onto our hard clay soil, and we soon discovered they grew just fine in the horrible growing conditions. In my garden journal, there's now a line about bok choi: "does fine in clay soil." Typically, in my journal, I use a list format. I note when I planted anything (seed or start), what variety it was, when it germinated or matured, when we harvested it, and if it did well. I try to note the weather, as I feel that helps, but often don't. Quick notes I can glance at are always helpful and serve to get me excited and motivated for the season ahead. Someday I'll have time to write more, but for now, this will do.

Variety Matters

If there was one piece of advanced gardening advice I'd advise you to think about, it's paying attention to the varieties of vegetables and flowers you're growing. If your goal is to replace the grocery store or market, there are specific varieties of each crop that produce more. If your goal is to minimize the need for pest control, there are varieties that are more pest- and disease-resistant for your specific climate and hardiness zone. If your goal is to maximize flavor, there are varieties that will suit your tastes best. After years of planting only what was easily available, I stumbled upon a spinach variety that did well for us, gave repeated harvests of huge leaves, didn't taste coppery, and made our cool season abundant. Now, it's the only spinach variety I need. I no longer have to think about which variety to grow as I've found my perfect match. I just throw its seeds into the garden each September. Take the time to experiment to find the varieties that suit you best; don't just grow whatever is on the shelves at your local hardware store.

I also like to grow many types of flowers, preferring long-stemmed varieties since they make it much easier to arrange and to gift. One huge and somewhat hidden benefit of the home garden is the ability to grow all the wild and wonderful varieties of plants that are uncommon and rare. This is one of the greatest joys of gardening—making the garden your own and getting to revel in the uniqueness that can only be done on a small scale. There are varieties of purple snap peas, orange and purple cauliflowers, pink celery, zinnias that look like dahlias, and rare plants you never knew existed. Lean into the privilege of getting to choose the varieties you grow and go buck wild.

Ten minutes a day keeps the pests away. Or at least it keeps the gardener sane!

Ten Minutes a Day

At the very minimum, an average-sized kitchen garden can be kept thriving with a mere ten minutes a day of focused energy. Twenty minutes is ideal for me and aligns with what doctors recommend for anyone hoping to manage stress through gardening. Go outside and set a ten-minute timer. See what you can do in that time frame, and I bet you'll be amazed at how you feel and what got done. Double that and you can call to thank me later.

What is most *useful* in this approach is the time you spend observing the garden, walking the paths, pinching and pruning as you go, staking a few things here and there, dropping some seeds in, and just doing a small amount every day. This ten-minutes-a-day approach avoids a "weekend crush" that turns into a four-hour sweat session where you come to realize half your tomatoes are rotting, a Japanese beetle mob has infested your corn, the peas aren't climbing, and powdery mildew is dusting the entire squash patch. I'm cranky just thinking about it. A little work at a time is far better than a crushing workload all at once.

Checking the garden daily is like taking a vitamin. It ensures that each day the bare minimum is met, and issues are seen as they arise, not when they hit their peak. And there is so much science behind this! Exposure to bright morning light sends a signal to your brain to suppress melatonin, your sleepy hormone, and engage serotonin, your happy hormone. Aligning your body's circadian rhythm with that of the sun helps you naturally be in a good mood. So, stack the habit of getting morning sunlight on top of your daily 10 minutes of gardening and it's like you double the benefit. Gardening has been proven to lighten mood, combat anxiety and depression, and give you the physical benefit of exercise. I don't know a single person who doesn't need this.

Start to pay attention, and you'll find each day is akin to an entire season. There is the dormancy of sleep (winter), awakening with the sun (spring), the busyness of the day (summer!) and then the calm and cozy wind-down before bed (autumn). Harmonizing tasks with the natural movement of the sun and moon allows us to function optimally. It makes sense that having a reason to get outside built into your day is about more than just growing more flavorful and nutritious food; it's rewiring us for health and happiness from the inside out.

CHAPTER 5

MAKE

After having my third child, the neighborhood we lived in got together and did a little meal-share program for us. People took turns delivering food to the doorstep or making something and dropping it off. We were grateful for every single gesture and felt truly loved. Though I will say, the older generation really knew how to do it. They always home-cooked something and dropped it off with a sweet note, a treat for the big kids, or a small vase of flowers and a little something extra for me. It was thoughtful and spoke to their own hearts as it warmed mine. Those gestures made a lasting impact, and I found myself asking for everyone's recipes. It connected us.

As I was growing up, craft fairs and homemade everything were very popular. My mother is incredibly crafty and creative and can sew and paint and make costumes—all of it. I was entirely charmed by it as a child, and then as an adolescent, I thought anything homemade was unbearable. I wanted *new* everything. Fancy everything. That was the year 2000 and new and fancy were in vogue. It was a time of plastic blow-up chairs and butterfly hair clips. Shiny and in-your-face pop culture was cool. Now, however, I am so grateful to have the skills my mother embedded in me: making tea, darning holes in sweaters, sewing dolls, and using felt to make Halloween costumes. In a world entirely filled with excess, making do is about more than the act of making. It's caring, thinking creatively, and knowing that convenience steals character, and ease is not always better.

In the kitchen garden are parallels. A handful of cherry tomatoes on a summer's day is all we need, not a big plastic clamshell full of gas-ripened fruit. Wandering out into the garden to find a rogue potato plant that yields two perfect spuds for the following morning's breakfast burritos makes us happy. There is a "just enoughness" in the garden, which you'll find quickly leaks into the rest of your home and the lives of you and your family. How can you make what you already have enough? And if you do need more, can you make it yourself? This chapter is about both. It's about making do with what you have, but it is also about making things yourself, like my mother did. And like I do, as much as I am able. I hope you find the following projects useful in your kitchen garden.

◄ A bouquet of flowers with some veggies from the garden mixed in offers a "surprise and delight" moment for the home.

New Beds

If there were one project to tackle in the kitchen garden that has the highest return on investment, it's building your own raised garden beds. Of course, you can buy raised bed kits online to be delivered within twenty-four hours, like most things; however, it's quite affordable and simple to make them yourself. There are dozens of plans and ways for doing so. Some are as easy as snagging some extra wood from a neighbor or pulling stones from your property to assemble something unique to you and your home. Others are more complex.

My husband and I built our very first raised beds with the help of a friend with a miter saw and we felt so entirely proud afterward. It's the pride of ownership you get after building your beds and the knowledge that you are capable of all sorts of things. Trust me on this one: Build your own raised beds if you can. Here's an easy way to do so.

RAISED BED BUILDING PLANS

The first step to take is to look at your garden's layout and design and determine the target size for your raised beds. Also consider your own size and style of gardening. The width of your raised beds should allow you to reach into the center of the bed easily. I am 5'9" (175 cm) tall and I can reach to the center of our 4-foot (122-cm)-wide raised beds easily. I also have a cap on the top of my beds so I can sit on the edge easily or set my coffee mug there. The children think this is for them to walk on of course, but it's also a pretty detail. You then need to think about the height of your beds. The taller the beds, the easier to sit on or bend over to tend to things, however the more soil you'll need to fill them and therefore the bigger the initial expense. Common raised beds sizes are 2 × 4 feet (61 × 122 cm), 3 × 6 feet (91.5 × 183 cm), and 4 × 8 feet (122 × 244 cm)—all nice tidy rectangles. Standard depths range from 12 to 24 inches (30.5 × 61 cm) and up. My personal raised beds are 4 × 8 feet (122 × 244 cm) and 18 inches (46 cm) deep, so we'll use that as our example.

Construction plans for a 4 × 8-foot (122 × 244-cm) raised bed

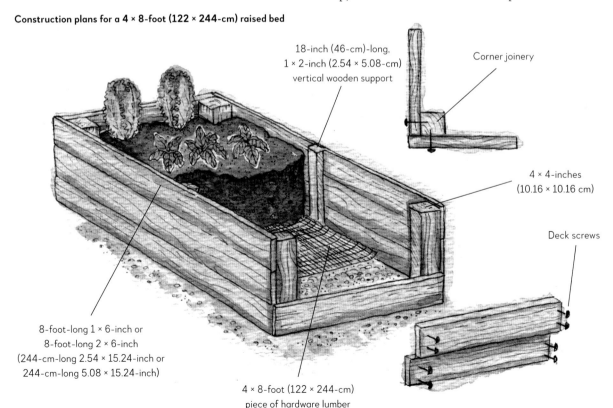

18-inch (46-cm)-long, 1 × 2-inch (2.54 × 5.08-cm) vertical wooden support

Corner joinery

4 × 4-inches (10.16 × 10.16 cm)

Deck screws

8-foot-long 1 × 6-inch or 8-foot-long 2 × 6-inch (244-cm-long 2.54 × 15.24-inch or 244-cm-long 5.08 × 15.24-inch)

4 × 8-foot (122 × 244-cm) piece of hardware lumber

The next consideration, after size, is material. Steel, aluminum, wood, and stone are the most common materials, though woven willow branches, called *wattle*, are also common, along with man-made items like cinder blocks or preformed landscape blocks. (Be very wary of found or chemically treated items, though, as they can contain lead or other toxins that you do **not** want leeching into your soil.) Within each category are a multitude of options and price ranges. I recommend going with what feels complementary to your home's style and/or personal style. Whatever lights you up and feels beautiful and sturdy is good enough, providing it is toxin free.

Raised beds typically have no bottoms. They are open so the soil below can be reached by plant roots. However, if your only option is to build your garden on a balcony, deck, or patio, you can use something with a bottom as your raised bed, like an old water trough. Just be sure there are adequate drainage holes.

If you opt for wooden beds, consider what type of wood to use and think about how long the wood will last. You want the most rot resistant you can afford. Pine, cedar, and redwood are common choices, listed here in order of least rot resistant, with redwood being the most resistant and often the most expensive. Choose "untreated" wood so that you know it's not been sealed or treated with anything toxic.

The other key component in designing your beds is support. The longer the raised bed, the more internal support it needs so the sides don't bow out. This is most important for wood and metal since rock won't have any issues with bending or warping due to pressure or heat. To make a simple wooden raised bed, follow the basics found in the accompanying illustration. Screw wood boards together, with a support at each corner joint to screw into. Plan to have small vertical wooden supports spaced every 3 to 4 feet (91.5–122 cm) along the length of the longest sides. Screw them on the inside of the long boards to keep the wood straight. You'll end up with a rectangular bed with internal corner supports and internal vertical supports to keep the bed sides from bowing, as pictured.

There are many ways to embellish these beds if you so wish, but if you want to add an edge cap like mine, it's quite simple. This thin piece of wood runs along the top of your raised bed so you can sit on it to tend to the garden. We used a ½-inch (1-cm) thick and 3-inch (7.5-cm) wide piece of redwood to cap our beds, cutting the ends on a diagonal so the result is mitered corners. They are attached to the beds' top edge with a couple of screws.

DIY Plant Markers

One finishing touch we love as a family are plant markers. Labeling plants is typically an afterthought, but it is a way to bring children into the fold after the excitement of planting has waned. I most love to make plant markers with wood and ink, though I often resort to writing in permanent marker on plastic or copper markers, if at all. This plant marker DIY is simple and easy, though they do need to be replaced each season.

Materials:

- Black ink pad
- Individual letter stamps
- Wooden plant markers, or pieces of wood with a flat side
- decoupage sealer (optional)

Instructions:

Use the letter stamps to write out the plant's name. The individual letter stamps can be used repeatedly, but they also make the activity fun (and educational!) for kids. Additionally, the typewriter look of the wobbly letters adds some homemade charm. To seal your wooden markers after the letters are added, add a swipe of decoupage sealer or even clear glue. This is not necessary, though water will likely ruin the ink over time.

Planting catmint for steams and teas.

Growing Tea

One of my very first and most exciting grow-it-myself and make-it-myself garden adventures was with tea. I went down the rabbit hole when I learned how tea bags are often bleached and many teas have chemicals and pesticides on them—all things I want to avoid. So, off I went to start growing my own tea. Growing tea is as easy as growing herbs, drying them, and then steeping them in water. Ah, the novelty!

Most commercial teas have either black, white, or green tea leaves as a base, with top notes of other plants layered in. Dried fruit, as well as spices, also make a fantastic complement to the herbs. While flavor is fun, we mostly use our homegrown tea to reap the homeopathic benefits. The children now know: a tummy ache begs for peppermint, and the worry bug (that's what we call anxiety for the little ones) can be kept at bay with some lemon balm and lemon verbena. Chamomile helps us relax and tulsi gives us clarity both mentally and physically (plus, it's great for loosening a tight chest in the winter).

However simple it may be, tea-growing has become a staple in my kitchen garden. While we don't grow black, white, or green tea leaves, our tea plants are herbs. They are unfussy to grow, with a few soil and water preferences depending on the plant. I recommend you sprinkle these plants into your garden beds, adding to the biodiversity of your garden, while also keeping some woodier herbs as perennial mainstays.

Tea Herbs to Grow in the Cool Season

- Rosemary
- Sage
- Thyme
- Tulsi
- Mint
- Lemongrass

Tea Herbs to Grow in the Warm Season

- Lemon balm
- Lemon verbena
- Tarragon
- Bee balm
- Chamomile
- Bergamot
- Basil
- Catmint

▶ Gathering homegrown herbs for tea is one of life's great joys.

DRYING HERBS

There are three ways to dry herbs for teas and other uses. Which method I choose all depends on my available time and the amount of effort I want to put in. The first method is simply bundling them up and hanging the bundles up to airdry in a warm, dry place. Make sure the bundles only have a few stems, so the air can circulate, and mold doesn't form. Additionally, remember to take the fully dried herbs down so that they don't gather dust. Most herbs should be dried out in about ten days when they are crunchy to the touch. Each season I inevitably forget about something drying and it becomes seasonal decor! Air drying retains the most oils and flavor in the plant, which is a huge bonus to using this method.

The second, and my preferred method for drying plants, is using a dehydrator. With a dehydrator, the plants become bone dry and don't gather dust. Plus, it's faster. I especially like to use the dehydrator for herbs to be used outside of the realm of tea: ones I'm bottling up for gifts or when I'm making something like red pepper flakes. I also use the dehydrator if I want to include a dried fruit or veggie, both of which really, *really* need to quickly dry, in the mix. This method only takes about a day—typically eight to twelve hours in the dehydrator depending on what you're drying.

The third method is oven drying. I personally use this method for one primary reason and that is to make herbed salts. However, it works for drying all herbs. For making things like chive salt (the secret ingredient in most of my cooking), blend the fresh herb with some big flaky salt and then dry it in the oven low and slow for about one to two hours (see recipe on page 151). You can also use the oven to dry plain herbs and fill the house with a yummy smell.

Once your herbs are dry enough to snap in your hands, they're ready to be stored. Airtight glass containers are my preference. Eventually you'll collect enough of these to have a little apothecary at your disposal.

Tea Blends and Benefits

These are four tea blends we frequently make and use in our home. The quantities per cup are a personal choice, but I consider one serving about 1 tablespoon (2 g) of dried tea leaves.

LEMON BALM & LEMON VERBENA TEA

Use a 1:1 ratio of dried leaves from both plants and even some flowers if the herb has matured. Steep with hot water and honey (optional).

I was first introduced to this blend by a dear friend and neighbor who was pregnant and having some anxiety and trouble sleeping. Her aunt sent her a baggie of dried lemon balm and lemon verbena for tea. I was having postpartum anxiety after my second child was born and so my friend gifted me some of those herbs. Just those two simple plants. I steeped them with some hot water and honey and did, in fact, feel the calm set in. This tea is by no means a replacement for getting professional help (which I also did), but it is a great way to support your nervous system.

CHAMOMILE MINT TEA

Blend two-parts dried chamomile to one-part dried mint for this tea.

This blend is perfect for after dinner when tummies are settling, and sleep is encouraged to come soon. Chamomile is like a gentle hug and a bedtime back tickle while mint soothes stomachs and helps move any discomfort through our system.

◄ Drying herbs on a ladder in the dining room.

Sage is a perennial in the garden and has many uses.

LEMONGRASS, RAISIN, ORANGE PEEL, AND VANILLA TEA

Combine 1 tablespoon (2 g) dried lemongrass, 1 teaspoon (3 g) raisins, 1 teaspoon (2.5 g) dried orange peel, and 1 teaspoon (2.5 g) dried vanilla bean powder.

This tea blend is inspired by a spa experience I had, thanks to my sweet husband. He sent me off for a massage after one particularly harrowing week of motherhood. They were serving this lemongrass vanilla tea, and I must have had four cups of it. It's uplifting and peaceful. Once home, I searched the internet for the blend and was able to find a recipe I adapted into this version. Enjoy!

CATMINT TEA

Use 1 tablespoon (2 g) of dried catmint.

Quite simple but impactful, catmint is a great tea for little ones who are under the weather. It's a great antiviral and antibacterial and tends to have a calming effect. When you feel like you just need to give comfort to a cold, this is an easy choice.

Herbal Steams

There are a few other must-use ideas for herbs that have become a part of my motherhood arsenal and help me feel equal parts Mother Mary and Stevie Nicks in a witchy-yet-maternal mix. I love to use these herbal remedies with the children because I believe it helps them be more in tune with their needs and know that reaching for synthetic medicine is not always the answer. Sometimes it's a gentle layering of plant medicine over time that helps us stay healthy, as opposed to a quick fix. Herbal steams are one of my favorites.

During cold season, herbal steams are a go-to. I pick fresh herbs, gently chop or crush them just enough to let the oils out, and then toss them into a giant pot of water with a lid. I bring the water to just-before-boiling, and then remove it from the heat, take off the lid, and place my face over the steam with a towel around my shoulders to keep the steam in. This can be done with children as well, though I recommend a smaller bowl and even less hot water (take care to be sure the children don't touch the hot water!). The herbs I use for a particular herbal steam vary based on the symptoms being experienced. I like tulsi for chest congestion, thyme for mucus, sage for a runny nose, and a mix of all three at times. They all have anti-inflammatory properties that gently soothe your cells. Sage is one to be wary of though, as it is drying, so breastfeeding mothers could experience some milk flow issues. Additionally, tuning in to your symptoms is helpful in choosing which herbs to use. I recommend doing additional research and getting advice from a medical professional or a well-trusted herbalist or naturopath when learning how this beautiful medicine can be best utilized.

COLD SEASON HERBAL STEAM RECIPE

Ingredients:

- A handful of tulsi, thyme, and sage

Method:

Fill a lidded pot with water about 3 inches (7.5 cm) high. Place herbs that have been gently bruised or crushed into the water and put the lid on. Bring the water to just above a simmer but below a boil. Remove the pot from the stove and place it on a heat-safe surface. Prepare yourself with a towel around your shoulders and remove the lid. Place your face over the pot, with a towel over your head to trap the steam. Be cautious so as not to burn your face with steam.

Kitchen Garden Flowers

The flowers growing in the kitchen garden can be useful beyond their beauty and pollinator support. Many are even edible. While you can grow absolutely any flowers you want in your kitchen garden, I prefer to keep bulbs, perennials, or any other plants you don't want to move, or those that are extremely viny or thorny, in borders and other areas not being seasonally turned or cultivated. Any edible flowers in the kitchen garden can be used as garnish for cocktails, cakes, and, of course, for floral arrangements.

A selection of edible flowers, including (clockwise from top left), nasturtiums, chamomile, pansies, chives, squash blossoms, lilacs, calendulas, and borage.

There is something enchanting about a flower you can eat. It cheers up every dish and drink it's a part of. It feels very *Alice in Wonderland* to eat something so pretty. Additionally, if you dig into flower meanings from the Victorian era, as well as the medicinal and meaningful uses of flowers in modern day times, you'll find an archive and history of charming antidotes and affections. If we're hosting people, there is not a single dish in my home that is not adorned with edible flowers; they make everything feel homemade and personal.

Many kitchen garden flowers are grown during the cool season. Pansies, violas, calendula, and stock are a few favorites. They make for fantastic garnishes and crafts when fresh and when dried. It can be a tad tricky to germinate the seeds of these plants, but it's worth the effort. For a brief period, I worked with a local nursery, helping them do social media, and while I was there, I was always asking questions about the flowers that were edible, but often not labeled as such. I wanted to know if they were treated with pesticides or chemical fertilizers. I was pleased to find out that many growers sell edible flower plants when they're simply too young to have been treated with anything. So, if you do buy these flowers at the nursery, they're often not marked as edible. I recommend you ask if they're organic or if they've been sprayed or treated with anything. And like all non-traditional "food" items, do your independent research on what is non-toxic and edible. Better to be safe (for example, sweet pea flowers are *not* edible, though sugar snap pea flowers are).

A Note About Perennials

One of the most beneficial acts we can take in the garden is to plant more perennials. Perennials are plants that regrow every spring, staying in the garden indefinitely. Annuals, on the other hand, live only one season then they need to be removed or composted. Typically, annuals bloom longer than perennials; however, perennials carry some important benefits. Since they're in the ground season after season, perennials don't disturb the soil and keep their carbon sequestered. All the good microbes and beneficial bacteria in the soil live undisturbed. Additionally, perennials are an important habitat for pollinators like native bees who need a place to overwinter. The year-round foliage of perennials, even if it has been frosted back, provides a home for many insects, as well as a food source. Many beneficial insects that help us control pest insects survive in companionship with perennials.

An example of this is with parasitic wasps, which do not sting humans and are a great friend to the garden. They prey on pests like caterpillars, aphids, and beetles, paralyzing them or laying their eggs in the adult or larva. Those eggs hatch and eat the host. Yikes! But, how amazing, right? The adult wasps feed on the nectar of many perennial flowers.

As you add to your garden year after year, weave in perennials as much as you can to up the ante. In doing so, you'll also cut down on the amount of work you have to do since you don't need to replant perennials every year or tend to them as much.

◄ Harvesting pansies for drying and decorating.

Artichokes are a great perennial to keep in borders because of their size and texture.

FAVORITE EDIBLE PERENNIALS FOR THE KITCHEN GARDEN

- Globe artichoke
- Rhubarb
- Radicchio
- Perennial kale
- Anise hyssop
- Bee balm
- Coneflower (Echinacea)
- Lavender
- Catmint
- Sage
- Yarrow
- Dahlia

Fresh-Cut Flowers

I remember in seventh grade there was an activity fair at my school and one of the stations was "The Art of Flower Arranging." I signed up because I love flowers, but remember thinking, "Someone needs to be taught this?" I thought you just placed the flowers in a vase and went on with your life. Of course, you absolutely can plop things into a jar and be on your merry way, but there are some good rules of thumb to follow for a better design, especially since the art of kitchen garden *living* takes the role of flowers in our lives much more seriously than a seventh-grade activity fair. I use flowers in my home in many ways and want to throw out some inspiration for you as well.

First and foremost, when it comes to seasonal home décor, nothing spruces up a space like a fresh bouquet. Plus, it's much cheaper than wallpapering a room that's feeling dumpy. Also, if you want to give your home a particular seasonal feeling, nothing quite does that like an in-season arrangement. Think holly clippings during the winter holidays and sunflowers in summer. It's a vibe.

Additionally, scent also provides so very much. The year's first sprig of jasmine is one I always bring in and place by the door. Everyone who walks by it gets a mood boost as they enter our home. Speaking of people coming into the house, guests almost always enjoy a fresh bouquet by the bedside as a quick and thoughtful way to welcome overnight company. I also love to pick one or two flowers for each of my children and leave a vase on the stairs or by their bedsides from time to time as a surprise. It's important for a child to know their loved one was thinking of them while they were away. Leaving a little bloom for them reminds them of that. These are the tiny moments that connect us to nature in ways we seldom think deeply about, and yet when they happen, we feel them so vividly.

FLOWER ARRANGING TIPS

When it comes to making a stunning arrangement, there are a few rules (perhaps more like suggestions . . . okay, *opinions*) I like to consider.

Height and Width

This is a method all the fancy florists use. The height of your bouquet should stand no more than two-thirds the height of your vase. For width, I find there are more liberties to be taken. A sprawling bouquet can be such a statement, and using things like honeysuckle to trail off the edge of a dresser brings a sense of life to the space. Play with everything, but try to have taller flowers in the center, at the back, or along the edges. Keep the shorter flowers in the front. The concept of "thriller, filler, and spiller" is used a lot when it comes to designing potted plants, but it applies to flower arrangements as well. A thriller is tall and large at the center of the vase, a filler takes up the middle space, and the spiller goes down over the edge. For vases, spilling over an edge can be a bit unkept looking, but sprawling outward at each side dances beautifully.

Pea vines make the perfect "spiller" for a floral arrangement.

Texture

I like to add texture to each arrangement, which can overlap with your surprise element (more on that in a bit). Something with a spiky texture among a jug of soft cosmos and daisies makes the whole thing really pop. Or you can have berried branches popping up through a cluster of roses. Little bumps, spikes (think thistle), reeds, and swirls. all add something interesting to give dimension to your gathering.

Surprise and Delight

If possible, add something unexpected to your flower arrangements like a branch of baby tomatoes or perhaps a colorful chard stem with a leaf still attached. Veggies in flower arrangements are one of my absolute most favorite delights (it's the little things in life). I also think a few stems of a native shrub or something colorful can spice things up, too.

Color

It's good to have a color scheme in mind when arranging flowers, though it's a very personal preference. I like to choose one color with a few variations, like deep, purply black foliage, lilacs, and a classic purple flower to make something fun to look at and easy on the eyes. Or I find a few flowers of the same general color and then layer in two more color options. Try to stay away from one-note coloring like all bright neon colors or all dark and moody colors. Adding a light cream to a dark arrangement only enhances the overall feel.

Scent

Like a house party where each guest wears a different perfume, a bouquet with competing scents can overwhelm. Pick one fragrant flower per bouquet if possible. Mixing scents can be challenging and some people are more sensitive to smells than others. Keep in mind that as the flowers age

◄ Flower arrangements with surprising pops of pea tendrils and rainbow chard are always a delight.

Stock is a lesser-known edible flower with a lovely fragrance.

and die, their smell will change too. It can be hard to pinpoint where bad smells are coming from (beyond the murky water in the bottom of the vase, of course).

Whether the art of arranging flowers is obvious to you or you're still learning, the main point is how lovely flowers make us feel. In Victorian times, flowers all had secret meanings and were often exchanged as a means of sending a message to someone that may not have been societally appropriate to share in person. I find that modern meanings assigned to flowers are just as impactful. Knowing someone's favorite flower and gifting them with a bouquet, or finding flowers that are named after loved ones and planting them in their honor are charming gestures. Use your space to add life to your home and to your relationships. Bring back the simple and nostalgic act of being thoughtful.

Using Edible Flowers

There are many ways to use edible flowers, but simply tossing them into a salad is one of the best gateway experiences. However, when it comes to edible flowers, your creativity should know no bounds. Once indoctrinated into the cult of flowers-you-can-eat, you'll never *not* be using them. We decorate cakes and cookies, as well as most dishes. A goat cheese flower log makes the Easter guests swoon. We love to use edible flowers for non-edible crafts, too. We've made them into bookmarks, turned them into gift tags, pasted them onto leaves and pumpkins, and transformed them into butterfly wings for dressing up. Many edible flowers have medicinal benefits and are useful for many ailments.

When using edible flowers as a decoration for things like breads, cakes, and cookies that are going to be baked with the flowers on them, it is best to press the blooms until they are at least half dry before exposing them to heat. If you don't, they'll shrink, and the colors will dull in the oven. Fresh flowers can work, but it's a bit of an art to know when to use the dry versus the fresh. Pansies and violas tend to hold up when baked fresh, but dianthus and chamomile get very small and withered, so I recommend drying those first and using an egg wash on top. For decorating food or garnishing it after it's cooked, both fresh and dried work well. When using edible flowers in herbalism or for medicinal practices, they often need to be made into an oil or distilled. You can explore many uses with things like tinctures, oxymels, teas, infusions, cordials, salves, poultices, and steams.

In the garden, edible flowers can often be great companion plants as they either attract beneficial insects or deter pests, while also beckoning in pollinators. Nasturtiums are a great trap plant as they attract aphids, keeping them from your other crops. Marigold is a great pest repellent as it has a strong fragrance that some pests don't like. Borage is another great edible flower that also

Nasturtium in bloom.

attracts and creates a habitat for beneficial insects like lacewings and parasitic wasps.

Most edible flowers, though wonderfully decorative, also have a distinct flavor. Pansies are a touch minty; nasturtiums offer a peppery flavor that can be quite strong; chamomile gives green apple flavors and scents; marigolds have their own musk; and borage brings a touch of cucumber flavor to the party. And don't underestimate what the scent of a flower does in your cooking and garnishing—it's a beautiful extra touch to place a nasturtium on top of a margarita for a little spice. It completely enhances the experience in a way that only gardeners can appreciate. As for the health benefits some edible flowers offer, there are flowers like calendula that have powerful anti-inflammatory and anti-viral oils within them, and flowers like pansies and borage that offer vitamin C, zinc, and iron. It's amazing to think about how these tiny flowers pack so much power in their beautiful petals.

While many edible and medicinal flowers are mild and gentle, some are not, and if used improperly, they can even be toxic. Consult an herbalist or doctor as you explore the uses and identification of these plants to be sure you're safe.

Pressing flowers in the pages of a book is as nostalgic as it gets. It's effective too!

PRESERVING EDIBLE FLOWERS

To best preserve edible flowers for baking, press them. This is different than drying because you want the blooms to lay flat and stay flat. If you simply dry them, they'll curl up and disintegrate. There is a place for simple drying like this when it comes to making teas, tinctures, and general herbal uses, but for edible flowers you want to look pretty, pressing is the way to go. You can be romantic and press them between the pages of a thick book, but I prefer to use a flower press. Presses you place in the microwave have become my preferred method. They are best at keeping the shape and color of the flower, as well as getting a very dry final product.

Common Medicinal Flower Uses & Benefits

While learning the medicinal benefits and uses of plants, keep in mind there is much research to be done. Get to know plants that are look-alikes, too, to help with proper identification. It's also important to track any reactions or allergies that could come about when using these plants, just like you would do for any type of food or medicine.

- **Echinacea** or purple coneflower is a well-known immune booster. It's great when you're feeling an oncoming seasonal illness. The root of this flower is what's most beneficial. It is dried and made into a tea.
- **Elderflower** has anti-inflammatory properties (it's great for tight sinuses) and is good at increasing immunity. Many people use elderflowers to make a cordial like St. Germaine, which is fun because it has detoxifying properties as well.
- **Calendula** is powerful for treating our skin, digestion, and immune system. For skin, calendula is a fantastic aid to any rash, sting, bite, or burn, including eczema (the salve recipe I share in the next section is a go-to for any of these). Calendula is a great plant for indigestion and tummy inflammation as well when used in tea form.
- **Rose** is a powerful plant for the skin and is a natural astringent and collagen-booster. It tightens pores and plumps fine lines. Rose water and creams are great for this. Rose is also known to help with menstrual cramps, as well as being mood-boosting when taken as a tea.
- **Chamomile** is widely known as a tea because it is great at relaxing your stomach post-meal, calming the nervous system to prepare for rest, and helping to soothe the stomach, whether it's from eating too much, too little, feeling nauseous, or just overall unsettled.

Calendula and chamomile salve is great for rashes, eczema, cuts, and scrapes.

- **Jasmine** is a mood booster and is used for stress reduction via breathing in the scent or using a hydrosol spray. Jasmine can also be soothing for psoriasis and dry skin when used in a bath.
- **Lavender** is well known for aiding sleep and fostering calm, but it's also fantastic for headaches, wound healing, and acne. Consider placing some lavender oil on your temples to ease tension or mixing some into a salve to soothe irritated skin.
- **Passionflower** is often used to treat sleeplessness and anxiety. It can also benefit people experiencing hyperactivity and restless minds. Tea is the most common way to use this great plant.
- **Violet** is a cooling, soothing, and anti-inflammatory plant. A violet poultice is lovely when used topically for bug bites and eczema.
- **Yarrow** used to be called *woundwort* because it's great at stopping nose bleeds, cuts, etc. When dehydrated into a powder or made into a poultice, it's a fantastic antimicrobial.

Calendula and Chamomile Salve

One summer, my children attended a Waldorf School camp with Miss Linnie (who I am convinced is a magical sprite who will one day simply turn into sparkles at the age of 210). Miss Linnie taught our family about "the healing basket" and we now have one at our house. The kids know to go and get the healing basket if anyone is hurt. It has all the equipment needed to care for scrapes, bruises, bites, burns, and cuts. In it, we keep some antiseptic spray that's all-natural but made for horses, as well as some homemade calendula salve. I make it in little tins, so we have a dozen of them to split amongst purses and cars, plus extras to give to anyone who needs it.

Calendula has useful antioxidant, antifungal, and wound-healing effects. Turning it into a salve is fantastic—it's like a hippie antibiotic ointment. I also use it as cuticle cream, for eczema, random itches, or anything we just can't (or don't want) to put a finger on. I added chamomile to this recipe because of its very calm impact and kind energy. It's like a mother kissing your ouchie in plant form.

CALENDULA AND CHAMOMILE SALVE RECIPE

Supplies:
- 1 canning jar with a plastic lid
- Cheese cloth
- Double boiler
- 1-ounce (28-ml) tins

Ingredients:
- About 2 cups dried calendula and chamomile flowers
- 1 cup (235 ml) almond oil
- 4 tablespoons (56 g) beeswax
- 2 tablespoons (27 g) shea butter

▶ Dried calendula, chamomile, beeswax, and shea butter is all you need to make a healing salve.

Method:

Pick and dry your flowers, making sure they are dry without any molding. Pack the dried flowers tightly into a jar and add almond oil, completely covering the flowers. Put the lid on the jar and let the mixture sit and infuse for a minimum of two weeks. The more time infusing, the stronger it will be. Once infused, strain the dried flowers out through a cheese cloth. What's left is calendula and chamomile oil, which can stand alone if you'd like. But to make it into a salve, mix the infused oil with the beeswax and shea butter. Pour the mixture into a double boiler over medium heat and stir constantly until melted. You don't want the oil to get too hot or you'll lose some of the medicinal properties. Once all the ingredients are melted, pour it into the tins and let it cool and solidify.

FOR THE LITTLE ONES

When growing vegetables, having children participate in seed sowing, harvesting, and all the fun helps them connect to their food. With herbal remedies, it's no different. Little ones are great at pouring oil into jars for infusions, picking flowers, and even laying flowers onto drying racks. No task is too small.

Homemade Gift Tags

It wasn't until adulthood that I really grasped the importance of a gift's presentation and the feeling of receiving something so beautifully thoughtful. My Aunt Carol wraps a gift so well that its mere presence makes you feel as though you've picked the golden ticket. Additionally, the homemade approach gives back to us in droves, filling our hearts with the beauty of the task itself. One such gesture lies in making sweet gift tags with dried flowers.

Many homemakers have a box with random yet useful cards and tags, saved for times of haste when a last-minute gift is needed. Of course, there's also the nefarious bag filled with gift bags that seemingly all mothers keep tucked away in a coat closet or laundry room, saving the pretty ones for reuse. Add pretty homemade tags to your arsenal of gift-giving things. They are just the personal touch needed to dress up any gift.

Never underestimate the power of a well-placed dried flower gift tag on a bottle of wine for a neighbor, on a teacher gift, or folded into a book with a note for your mother-in-law: simple, thoughtful, elegant. To make these gift tags, you only need three or four items, all of which you

Pasting dried flowers onto gift tags.

FOR THE LITTLE ONES

Children are the best pickers of flowers and love this task. Send them out to hunt for things based on color, shape, size, and quantity. They'll be busy for gobs of minutes, and if your children are still little, consider sitting for a hot cup of coffee while they daydream and pick daisies for you. Be sure to instruct or demonstrate the stem length that you want, as overzealous helpers often come home with just petals or only a flower head.

may even have on-hand. You'll need pre-made tags from the store, or some thick card stock cut into your desired shape with a hole punched in (I love the classic rectangle with the corners cut off), string or ribbon to create the fastener, dried flowers, and glue or decoupage sealer.

Once the string is added to the tag, arrange the dried flowers onto the tag until you're happy with the design. Then, brush a thin layer of glue onto the back of each flower so it stays in place as you complete the next step. Let the glue dry and then cover the entire tag and all the flowers with a thin layer of glue to create a covered and slightly glossy finish while protecting the flowers. Try to leave the other side of the tag clean so you can write your sweet nothings and endearing notes on it.

Floral Ice Cubes

Another fun edible flower craft I always have on hand are floral ice cubes. Children delight in this fancy touch with their lemonade, and a carrot margarita with chamomile ice cubes is the ultimate cocktail moment for grown-ups. To make these stunning ice cubes, I recommend using ice molds that are square and or other fun shapes, as the classic half-oval ice cube doesn't land as nicely. However, the shape is less important than

what's inside. Start by rinsing your edible flowers to be sure no bugs or dirt are lingering. Next, fill your ice trays with water. Place the flowers in and push them gently with a fork so they're pressed against the edges and bottom of the cubes as much as possible. You want the face of the flower to be close to the edge of the cube, so it's visible in your drinking glass, but still covered with water to freeze properly. Freeze and enjoy.

FAVORITE EDIBLE FLOWERS

- Nasturtium
- Butterfly pea flower
- Borage
- Pansy
- Chamomile
- Snapdragon
- Stock
- Calendula
- Chive blossoms
- Dianthus
- Marigold
- Chrysanthemum
- Daisy
- Dahlia
- Primrose
- Rose
- Magnolia

DIY Pest Prevention and Control

Growing up in Northern California when I did, there was a mix of hippie commune culture, Silicon Valley early-adopter wealth, wine industry affluence, and agricultural blue-collar families. It made for an interesting upbringing full of characters whom I adore. It also made me what I call "crunchy-ish." Being "crunchy" is derived from the anecdotal granola-eating hippie. Being crunchy means you're sort of anti-Western medicine and a bit counterculture. So, I call myself crunchy-ish, hence all the herbal remedies. Making your own fertilizer spray and employing natural pest prevention methods is another way of flexing those crunchy muscles and doing things the natural way. Synthetic chemical fertilizers, much like synthetic food, are poor for the environment and for the good bacteria in the soil, as well as for the overall health of pollinators and plants. No actions in nature are one-off. Every gesture is an extension of the whole.

It is also such a power move to have these self-reliance tools at our fingertips. "The disease is the remedy" is a saying that comes to mind, reminding us that looking within the garden for answers can be the best solution to what's ailing her. There are many ways to enhance the natural benefits of many plants and reposition them to work for us. Like when you companion plant, using strong natural scents is huge for deterring pests in the garden. Garlic spray and peppermint are two tried and true methods for keeping critters at bay. Garlic, onion, marigold, mint, and pepper are all great natural pest deterrents. Here are some home remedies I use and swear by.

PEPPERMINT DIFFUSERS FOR RAT REPELLENT

Urban gardens are notorious for harboring these rodents. I once found a small family of rats sleeping under my overgrown comfrey plant and to this day, I get the creeps when I'm in that part of the garden. Beatrix Potter made critters in the garden seem so endearing and cute; she built us a bed of lies! It was not cute, and I was not endeared.

Materials:

- Small 3-ounce (89-ml, approximately) containers with lids (baby food storage containers work well)
- A roll of candle wick
- Peppermint oil (get the cheap stuff in bulk)

Method:

Poke a hole in each lid that's large enough to pull a piece of the wick through, then set aside. Fill each container ½ to 1-inch (1–2.5-cm) full of peppermint oil and place the lid back on. Next, stick the end of the wick down through the hole until it dips into the peppermint oil and reaches the bottom of the container. Trim the upper end of the wick so 1 inch (2.5 cm) of wick is sticking out above the lid. Now you have a little peppermint oil diffuser to place outside in the garden. I like to put six in each 4 × 8-foot (122-cm × 244-cm) bed (one per 4 square feet [3716 cm^2]) to deter rats.

GARLIC SPRAY

This spray is fantastic as an aphid and slug deterrent, as well as to keep powdery mildew and vampires at bay. Kidding about the vampires (mostly).

Materials:

- Spray bottle
- 1 head garlic
- 8 ounces (240 ml) water

Placing a brick on some comfrey to use as a fertilizer.

Adding water to the comfrey to let the plant soak and breakdown.

Method:

Blend a head of garlic with the water in a blender or food processor and pour the mixture into a spray bottle. You want the garlic pureed as smoothly as possible, so it doesn't clog the spray bottle. The infused water is what we really want to get onto the plants. That's it!

COMFREY FERTILIZER

Comfrey is a wonderful plant for remediating soil and adding both nitrogen and potassium to it. You can even be a bit laissez-faire and chop down comfrey leaves and let them sit and decompose into the soil naturally, acting as a living/dying soil amendment. Comfrey plants live for years, so find it a happy home somewhere in the garden and make use of it. Comfrey tea fertilizer is a great way to capitalize on all that nutrition, and making it is quite simple.

Materials:

- 5-gallon (19-l) bucket with lid
- Brick
- Water
- Comfrey leaves

Method:

Cut off a bunch of comfrey leaves and place them into the bucket. Squish the leaves down and top them with a brick to keep them compressed at the bottom of the bucket. Aim for ⅔ full or less. Fill bucket the rest of the way with water and close the lid. Keep the bucket somewhere out of the way for about six weeks. The result is a potent fertilizer "tea" you can use to increase the amount of nitrogen and potassium in your soil in a form that is easy for your plants to uptake.

The *living* part of a kitchen garden—the infusing of the garden into your life—is often the hardest part. Modern conveniences make things like herbal steams feel slow to work or the act of pressing flowers feel cumbersome when you could have some perfectly dried and pressed blooms delivered to your door in a day. However, heading to a pharmacy or clicking an order button doesn't arm you with the secrets to good health like using herbs and flowers you grew yourself does. Convenience can't build character and unwind you from the stress of the day like the simple work of your own fingers in a project. Don't get so busy building and maintaining a garden that you forget to enjoy the many fruits of it.

CHAPTER 6

GATHER

In my family, food is taken very seriously—and taken *everywhere* with much seriousness. My stepfather taught me how to cook bacon-wrapped quail in a Dutch oven over a fire while we were tent camping. My mom will throw another Dutch oven on top of that for her meatloaf and another Dutch oven on top of that for some chocolate lava cake. We. Don't. Play. When it comes to food—anything, anywhere, as long as it's gourmet.

One summer weekend in college, I went to visit my Aunty Pammy so we could all go up to the lake and camp. She and my Uncle Lee had a property where they built an outdoor kitchen that was powered by electricity via a generator. They were a wine-industry family, so food and beverages were taken very seriously (as they should be). Uncle Lee would pull out one of their award-winning pinot noirs that he had casually clinking around in the back of his bright red Jeep (a Jeep that I, as a child, would hang onto for dear life as he plummeted us to our near-deaths up and down the forested hills of a town called Cazadero).

When I arrived at Pammy's house for this visit, she promptly sent me outside to harvest basil. This was far before I had grown anything of my own. I shot her an uncertain look. Certainly, this wasn't a lake-trip priority? Oh, I was wrong. She took me out with some clippers and a basket, showing me how to take just the top quarter of the basil stem, just above a set of leaves so she can get more out of the plant in a few weeks (as opposed

to clear-cutting it). "When it's ready, it's ready. We have to harvest the basil, or it will bolt, and we'll lose our pesto opportunity," she explained. I didn't understand it at the time, but I went with it. I harvested basil until my fingertips were stained a yellowish green.

We subsequently loaded all the basil, a huge food processor, and a vacuum sealer into the back of her Suburban, alongside our bathing suits and coolers full of ice. We, of course, also brought along loads of garlic, pine nuts, parmesan, and olive oil. Sure enough, we blended up pounds and pounds of fresh pesto right by the campfire. We set up a whole station and everyone took turns prepping garlic, running the food processor, scooping the pesto into bags, and labeling and vacuum sealing them. We froze the pesto, and everyone took some home.

This is part of the beauty of life in the kitchen garden. It's a dedication to your harvests, knowing that if you miss the opportunity, Mother Nature will keep moving without you. Some plants, if left in the ground and not harvested, eventually bolt (flower and set seed), which means they will be pushed into the next phase of their lifecycle. Once plants bolt, their energy moves from leaves to flowers. In the case of plants with edible foliage, bolting changes the taste of the plant, typically making it more bitter. This is why Aunty Pammy needed to process her basil—it would have gone into the next phase of its life, and we wouldn't have been able to enjoy a winter's worth of pesto.

◄ Eating seasonally means letting the garden dictate what's for dinner.

In the garden's beauty there is so much enrichment. This is the magic, the satisfaction. This is where you look at your life and add in resilience—self-reliance. I'm sure Pammy looks back on this and smiles, not thinking much of it, but it left a mark on me because it was so enchanting. It added a layer of life to our trip, a sense of purpose and fun that is deeply felt when you work with your hands for the greater good. There we were, heaving a food processor out of the car when everyone else was throwing sleeping bags around. We did that too—we went out on the Jet Skis and slept under the stars in our tents—but we also all worked at something together and it was so *worth* it.

This all brings me to the *how* of the harvest. There is a right time to pick herbs, fruit, and vegetables, gathering it all up for immediate and future use. In this chapter, we'll explore how to harvest and preserve the garden's offerings, an essential step in the kitchen gardening process that is often overlooked and underestimated.

How to Harvest

Plant by plant, there is a way, whether intuitive or not, to pick vegetables and herbs. There are seven common classifications of vegetables: root vegetables (beets, carrots), stem vegetables (asparagus, celery), edible tubers (potatoes), leaf vegetables (lettuces), bulb vegetables (onions), head or flower vegetables (broccoli and cauliflower), fruits that are considered vegetables based on use (cucumber, tomato), and seed vegetables (peas, beans). Can we take a moment to be cheesy and astounded that the diversity of vegetables is just so magnificent? So much variety! Okay, resume reading.

Each vegetable is harvested a bit differently and much of it you'll intuit simply by knowing what they look and feel like when you purchase them from a farmer's market. But I have some harvesting tips to make your garden shine and provide much more than you'd otherwise think.

Young basil plants just a couple of weeks away from harvesting.

Harvesting purple Beauregarde peas.

▶ Harvesting lettuce with the cut-and-come-again method.

CUT AND COME AGAIN

For herbs, lettuce, and leafy greens, it's best to harvest at whatever stage of maturity you prefer, but harvesting in the cut-and-come-again style means you harvest a little bit of the plant (a few leaves) at a time and leave the rest of the plant intact so you can harvest again and again. It's important to prepare for this at the beginning of the season so you have enough plants in the ground to take some leaves from each, giving you the yield that you desire.

For lettuce, take a few outer leaves from each plant. For basil, top each stem off as it matures, leaving a few sets of leaves at the bottom so side shoots can grow, and you can keep harvesting. All herbs thrive when regularly harvested, so aim to take the top third of the plant and let the rest keep growing. For leafy greens like swiss chard or spinach, the plant can be eaten as baby greens or when it's more mature. With chard you can even eat the stalks, much like celery. Most leafy greens, including bok choi, kale, and arugula, should be treated this way. Broccoli is an odd plant and can be treated as cut-and-come-again by harvesting the main head of florets and then allowing side shoots to form.

CUT-AND-COME-AGAIN PLANTS

- Arugula
- Basil
- Chives
- Bok choi
- Beet greens
- Radicchio
- Lovage
- Green onions
- Most herbs
- Kale
- Lettuce
- Mustard greens
- Nasturtium
- Parsley
- Celery
- Lettuce
- Spinach
- Swiss chard

As for herbs, there are soft-stemmed herbs and woody herbs. Rosemary is an example of a woody-stemmed herb. As rosemary matures, the stems get harder and larger near the base, but the new growth at the top comes in soft. To harvest plants like this (rosemary, thyme, tarragon), cut the new shoots right where the woodiness meets the softness. You can also propagate these plants, placing the soft-bottomed cutting into a jar of water. It will form roots after about ten days. The cutting can then be transplanted into soil for an entirely new plant.

When harvesting soft-stemmed herbs like basil, parsley, and cilantro, leave some of the growth intact. Basil stems have leaf couples, which are pairs of leaves that grow opposite each other on the stem. Try to cut basil shoots just above two sets of couples if you can and new shoots will soon emerge.

HARVESTING BY CLASSIFICATION

While leaf vegetables can be harvested either cut-and-come-again style or as whole mature vegetables, other classifications of vegetables require different harvesting techniques.

- **Root vegetables** are harvested all at once by pulling up the entire plant. A beet, for instance, is pulled up, with the beetroot being what you're eating (though the greens are edible too). These are easy—pull them up and you're done.
- **Stem vegetables** can sometimes be cut and come again and sometimes be taken all at once. Whatever your preference. I have some fennel I've fully harvested all at once and it is now growing back because I left the root in the soil to regrow. However, I could also pull the plant all the way out and make space for something new in the garden.
- **Edible tubers** are fun because once you grow them, you will never *not* grow them (little gardener joke). Tubers like potatoes spread underground, making it hard to completely

harvest them all. Some always get missed and resprout the following year. Fine by me. For edible tubers, gently harvest them once their above-ground greens and flowers have died back to brown foliage. Then take a garden fork and gently dig them up.

- **Bulbs** are harvested all at once. This includes onions and garlic. Pull them up and eat (or store) the bulbs. Easy peasy. You'll know they are ready for harvest when the foliage has partially died back. For onions, the green tops should be yellow and flopped over entirely. For garlic, the bottom six leaves should be yellow or brown before the garlic bulbs are gently pulled up or forked out.

- **Head vegetables** are clusters of flower buds. Broccoli, cauliflower, and artichokes are examples of this. You harvest the head (though the leaves make a fantastic base layer on a cheese or charcuterie board) by cutting it from the plant.

- **Fruits** that are commonly treated as vegetables are tomatoes, cucumbers, eggplant, zucchini, peppers, squash, pumpkins, and avocados. They all have flesh surrounding their seeds, which makes them fruit (by a botanist's standards), but we use them like vegetables and grow them with other veggies. Fruits like these are best harvested when they are ripe. As you harvest them, the plant then grows more until the weather stops cooperating. Harvesting fruits as they ripen keeps the plant producing. Some fruits do well counter-ripened and can be harvested early, just as they start to ripen. For example, a blushing tomato that is just starting to turn red can be picked and taken inside to fully ripen, signaling to the plant to grow more and also keeping the ripening fruit safe from pests.

- **Seed vegetables** are those grown for their edible seeds or pods. Peas and beans are in this category. As you've learned, when a plant goes to seed, it's nearing the end of

My six-year-old helping pick peppers. Little ones love to help harvest!

its lifecycle. Harvest the pods and seeds as often as you can so the plant gives us more goodies. However, if you're growing beans for dry storage, those can be left on the plant to dry on the vine and then be harvested in their dried shells. If you want to enjoy beans fresh (like green beans), then get out there daily to harvest and keep the plant producing.

FOR THE LITTLE ONES

Children love to harvest things because pulling anything out is wildly satisfying. Start with supervised harvesting, helping them learn the difference between "ripe" and "not ready yet." Once they gain some independence, lean into the two-hand harvesting system so they don't accidentally rip up an entire plant while pulling off a pea pod. As they get older, quiz your kids, and build their plant identification skills as you send them out to retrieve dinner ingredients.

When to Harvest

First, let's talk about flavor. There's a term I learned from my dear college friend Boo Simms, who owns a cheese and charcuterie shop with her twin sister (enough said, right?). The term is *flavor gap*. Often, the food we buy at a grocery store has been store- or truck-ripened and grown in depleted soil. There's also a good chance it's bland and water laden. Chefs go to great lengths to find the best produce at farmer's markets or from small growers because the produce they source has proven to be more flavorful. That gap between what we grow in our home gardens and what is available in the produce section is called the flavor gap. Oof, right?

In addition to the gorgeous, healthy, brimming-with-good-microorganisms soil we gardeners have, we also have fruits and vegetables that are ripened by the sun, irrigated by clean water, and grown with other plants that complement them. So, "peak ripeness in peak season" is our superpower. This is both for flavor and for health benefits. Not all superheroes wear capes. Some of us don dirt under our fingernails and jeans stained by worm poop.

Each plant prefers to be harvested at a certain time of day. Tomatoes are best when still warm from the sun.

RIPENESS

If flavor is your main target when navigating the best harvest time, know that it's you who decides when flavor is at its peak. Do you want baby plants with a soft taste, perfectly ripe and at peak performance? Or do you want mature vegetables that provide more food or, in some cases, stronger flavor? Smaller leaves tend to be milder in flavor (think baby arugula), larger leaves more flavorful, and flowers *most* flavorful. As your plants mature, the flavor changes. In root vegetables, as they age, the sugars develop, making them sweeter. With greens, as they age, bitterness develops. And things like squash and tomatoes get larger and often waterier in flavor as they age. The level of desired ripeness is all up to you.

TIME OF DAY

The last consideration to account for is what time of day to harvest your plants. I'm not trying to micromanage your schedule, so do as you please,

Tomatoes can be pulled off the vine early to ripen inside, but letting them fully ripen on the stem makes for the tastiest option.

but it's best to get out and harvest fruits, leafy greens, and stem vegetables in the morning when the plant is full of water and not stressed. They've not yet been taxed by the wilting sun.

For roots, edible flowers, and seeds, I like to snag these when the morning dew has evaporated and the day is warmer, so they aren't weighed down by any lingering moisture and *are* full of some of that life force energy from the sun. Though, of course, if you were at my home, I can be seen gathering my harvest about thirty minutes before dinner and then dashing out again a mere five minutes before dinner is pulled from the stove, adding my final aromatics and herbs. That mad dash is one of my favorites—it's that final thought of, "Oh, this will make things sing!"

When to Rip Out Plants

Pulling out plants becomes easier the farther along you are in your gardening journey. For the first two years, I was altogether precious about this. I mourned the final moments with my tomatoes. Now, I am ruthless. I'm like a greedy Grim Reaper with my scythe. When a plant's time is up, it's up. Nothing stays unless it's a perennial that's healthy, producing now or in the future, and not causing garden drama like harboring pests or powdery mildew. This is somewhat subjective of course, but I want to touch on something perhaps controversial. Many folks believe pulling plants out by the root is depleting the soil and harming the delicate web of microorganisms below, so they never pull plants up by their roots, instead opting to cut them off at soil level. However, there are pests and diseases that can live and ruminate in the soil, causing future problems. So, it's a judgment call. For a hardworking kitchen garden, space is typically limited, and plants are being rotated out as they complete their life cycle. We need the space to grow new food, so I, and many other kitchen gardeners, do often take entire plants out by their roots. For shallow-rooted

plants like lettuce, it can be easier to "chop and drop," which means to cut the plant off at the base and then let the dead plant and intact root system naturally decompose where they are. However, this can be unsightly and may harbor bad pests, like slugs and pill bugs. Because we know so much about the environment, modern gardening can present you with moments like this where each gardener must decide what is important to them. I tend to do a combination of both, leaving some roots and pulling up others, depending on the health of the plant I'm pulling out, the health of the soil, and which plants are going in as subsequent replacements.

An additional point of discernment pertains to seed saving. It is wise to grow enough plants to allow at least a few to go to seed, allowing you to not only save the seeds for next season, but also to let birds and other wildlife benefit from them. No plant will be better suited for your garden than one that has come from a mother plant who did well in it. With each saved seed comes the inherited "plant wisdom" and ever-so-slight adaptation to its most recent setting. The more and more you save your own seeds, the better adapted your plants will be to your micro-climate and ecosystem. It is additionally lovely to witness the full lifecycle of your vegetables, watching how quickly or quietly they mature, what their flowers and seed pods look like, and so on.

Each year there are many "volunteer" plants popping up in my garden (meaning plants that self-sowed and found their own time and place in the garden). I love to take note of when and where a volunteer plant grows, as opposed to when I'm the one who placed it. Tomatoes pop up year-round for me. However, I know these volunteers won't produce or stay as healthy as when I direct-sow them in the ground in April or May. Nasturtium is another plant I learned did much better in my cold season after observing the plant thriving with ease and popping up through my pea gravel in November.

There is a level of surrender that's rewarded in the kitchen garden, teaching us new ways to pay attention and be flexible—yielding to nature instead of white knuckling our schedules and planting plans. However absolutely played out and annoying the sentiment: It is, in fact, the journey that is as important as the destination. With any luck, each spot along the path becomes a destination. Some truths you cannot escape.

Preservation

I'm sure the Garden of Eden was expertly mapped out and succession sowed, leaving Adam and Eve with a continuous yield year-round. However, the darned snake and the apple and all that jazz ruined everything and now we must deal with gardens capable of producing too much or too little.

In warmer climates, you may be able to keep the garden going year-round (we do!). A year-round garden is about using what you grow often and easily, as well as finding short-term storage techniques like freezing and quick pickling. If your growing season is short, grow and harvest as much as you can and store the bounty in various fashions to be enjoyed throughout the year. Canning can be your best friend, along with freeze-drying, freezing, and dehydrating. A root cellar is fantastically useful.

Canned goods are a staple in the kitchen garden home, helping us be a good steward of our harvests.

Of course, each plant has its own best way of being preserved and used. Your time and financial commitments are other factors to consider. I employ a myriad of techniques for making use of all the goodness from my kitchen garden and find that during the peak of our warm season, when I am busy managing the garden, I can't keep up with the preserving. Tomatoes are a great crop to freeze whole and tackle later, during the cool season, when life has calmed a bit, and the kids and I need an indoor task to keep us from going insane on a rainy day.

CANNING, FREEZING, DRYING, AND STORING

These four horsemen of food preservation—canning, freezing, drying, and storing—are go-tos that keep a kitchen gardener sane on their quest to rely less and less on the grocery store. Let's look at the benefits of each, and then use this to inform what needs to be prepared in advance of harvest.

Curing and Storing

I'll never forget the first year I was fully able to replace what I would normally buy at the grocery store with my homegrown vegetables. I filled an entire raised bed with onions—sourced from a mix of plugs from an onion farm in Texas—and was absolutely thrilled to get my family out to see them plumped up, sitting on the soil. When they're ripe, onions appear to just be placed on top of the soil with their bulbs all full and gorgeous and their green tops now brown and flopped over. They look desperate to be pulled up. Even my darling golf-loving husband from the suburbs of Illinois was quite blindsided by how his wife took a turn toward *Little House on the Prairie* with her new, all-consuming passion. Even *he* was out there bright-eyed and in awe of these onions! "Babe, these are real onions!" Yes, my love, quite real. I was proud as punch as the kids took turns pulling onions up, filling two huge boxes. We had eighty onions! That's surely enough for the year. I had done it. I had achieved gold status as a home gardener.

And then I ruined nearly half of them (okay, I'll be honest—maybe more than half).

So, what happened? I didn't dry or cure them before storage. Onions need to be cured and properly stored, especially in a climate like mine that is humid at times and without a cellar or basement. Curing prevents rot by creating a protective skin. Onions need airflow and their skins need to harden, and I just didn't manage them well. I shudder with a bit of shame about this because I sort of knew I needed to do this, but I let life take my time over and thought I could cheat the system. Alas, you cannot. At least now I can hope to save *you* from the heartbreak.

To cure onions and garlic, carefully harvest them and do not puncture their skin (Same goes for potatoes and sweet potatoes.) Let them sit out in dry, covered, and well-ventilated conditions until the necks are hard and tight—about two weeks. Then move them into long-term storage that's darker and cooler, but still well ventilated. Do not wash these veggies as it creates too much moisture. If you feel you must wash them, do so at the time of cooking.

Dried beans and peas need to dry and cure in their pods before being stored. You can often let them dry on the vine, but if you have a lot of rain, they can mold. To dry and cure them off the vine, wait to harvest until the pods are fully browned and papery. Pick them before they crack open. Keep the pods warm and dry for about two weeks to properly cure, then open the pods and remove the seeds. Store them in a glass jar with a lid or a paper bag.

Canning

Ah, the pièce de résistance: canning. There is water bath canning and pressure canning, and they both require supplies and have a bit of a learning curve (though it's much easier than you may think if you're a first timer). If you want to store a lot of foods prepared from the garden, such as marinara, salsa, pickles, jam, and applesauce, then you need to get into canning. The bible of all canning resources comes from the Ball Canning company (*Ball Complete Book of Home Preserving*), and I highly recommend you lean into that resource. You'll need a basic knowledge of how to use pectin, how to determine the acidity in each vegetable/fruit, and which method is best for your desired outcome. Pressure canning is for low-acid foods and water bath canning is for high-acid foods. The acidity can be naturally occurring or added in (as with pickling). I highly recommend learning to can your produce, but there are also other, easier, methods to preserve your harvest.

Freezing

Freezing is the fastest way to get produce out of the kitchen and store it for later use. For traditional freezing, you can freeze items whole but know their texture often changes. Something like a tomato, because of the water within, will lose some of its firmness. Purees freeze beautifully, and flash freezing anything you want to stay intact is fabulous. We make a lot of breakfast burritos and so we dice up onions, potatoes, and peppers for that purpose. I cut everything up and freeze it overnight on a cookie sheet, so each individual piece freezes separately (this is called flash freezing). Then mix the frozen items together in a bag to be pulled from weekly without having a large frozen clump you need an ice pick to dismantle.

Many vegetables need to be blanched in boiling water prior to freezing to maintain their color and texture. Dunk broccoli, kale, cauliflower, green beans, and other washed and chopped produce into a pot of boiling water for 2 to 3 minutes before transferring them into an ice water bath to quickly cool down. Drain and pat off the excess water, then pack the veggies into labeled freezer bags.

Freezing stock is an easy way to preserve a staple ingredient.

Drying

As with tea herbs, there are many ways to dry food. You can bake, dehydrate, hang-dry, or even sun-dry many different vegetables. Freeze-drying is another option, though it requires special equipment. Freeze-drying captures flavors and nutrition well by reducing the water content as much as possible—close to 99 percent. Freeze-drying allows for storage up to about twenty-five years, while more traditional drying methods preserve food for only about one year by removing about 70 to 90 percent of the moisture.

STORING ROOT VEGGIES

Depending on where you live, you may have a root cellar or basement. Or perhaps you can grow year-round and don't really need much storage. Regardless, if you do decide to grow a bumper crop of root veggies, storing them properly is necessary.

Potatoes, sweet potatoes, and onions (all unwashed) require cool, dry conditions with ventilation for long-term storage. Cardboard boxes with holes throughout or mesh onion bags work well. Try to avoid humidity or these roots will either rot or form eyes and shoots.

Carrots, beets, and parsnips need to be stored in a cool, dry place such as a basement, root cellar, or garage. They should be unwashed and sealed in a container filled with sawdust or some moist sand. Space the roots so they are not touching.

The Art of Gathering People with a Purpose

Much like the beauty of a full harvest basket coming into the kitchen, a full home filled with people and love is part of what makes a kitchen garden so satisfying. Sharing the bounty with others and nourishing them with your soulful, flavorful, wildly more healthy food is what it's all about. Send guests and children out to harvest before dinner and find your home calling people in for a lifetime.

Every fall my family used to host an elk hunt in Montana. It sounds quite fancy, but it was really a bunch of us piled into my father's log cabin in the snow, sleeping in canvas bedrolls by the fire, and staying up late showing off our moonwalking skills. We took turns cooking and telling stories, and by the end of the trip, my dad had usually snuck a few pounds (about 1.36 kg) of frozen elk into my carryon luggage (yes, that's legal and never thawed during the five-hour travel day).

I spent a couple of years hoarding my wild game, moving it from apartment to apartment with me, obnoxiously filling the shared freezer space in the tiny fridge I shared with a roommate. Finally, after moving in with my husband, I felt the time had come to cook the elk—it was for the first party we threw as a couple for the Super Bowl. I made elk sliders, and they were a raging success. Not only did they taste amazing, but the guests were wildly impressed by the game and enthralled by the stories of the elk hunts. This was my first taste of the joy of sharing something more meaningful than a veggie tray from the grocery store.

Food tells a story, and sharing it always sends a sweet message. The kitchen garden is our greatest accomplice in this, and in fact, half of the glory is in the gifting and gathering. My secret ingredients are always some sort of herbed salt and my go-to appetizer for guests is a flower-adorned goat cheese log dripping in honey. Truly, finding ways

Gathering for a gathering—get your loved ones together and treat them to good food.

to surprise and delight company with something simple but homegrown will forever be my favorite party trick. Throwing some sprigs of chamomile on top of a tray of beans or a few marigolds beside some burritos dresses up the most ordinary meals when you're feeding a casual crowd.

I fear the art of gathering is getting lost as our world dives deeper into technology and our generation's devotion to escaping life rather than pouring into it grows. Assembling people is more important now than ever, to not only escape what is being called a "loneliness epidemic," but also to preserve the old ways of celebrating life and sharing the wisdom and comfort of that. In this chapter, we'll explore activities to welcome others in and ideas for hosting, as well as a few ways to create a welcoming home. The history of the kitchen garden shows us how important the role of sharing is and how a shared labor makes a task unburdened.

HOST A SEED SWAP

There was a thrilling online seed exchange I participated in two years in a row; it was such a delight. I was sharing about gardening online and most of my "gardeny" friends were virtual friends spread around the country. Most I'd met through my blog. One woman sorted and matched us all up by hardiness zone and interests, and then we all sent a package to one person, while also receiving a package from another. These packages were filled with garden goodness and homemade items. They were the sweetest, most thoughtful gifts. It was a true thrill and delight.

Each package was unique and most had gifts in them, like a wildflower seed mix, a favorite package of beans, cute tea towels, a wooden mason bee home, some beeswax food wrappers, homemade jam, and so on. Our exchange was through the mail, but an in-person seed exchange is the perfect activity for a gathering as you gear up for a new season in the garden.

Gather seeds to share at a seed swap and note the collection date, plant, and variety.

There is, of course, more than one way to host a seed swap. I'll share two approaches. The first is much like the American tradition of "Secret Santa." Gather a group of friends (and friends of friends!) and fill out a casual About Me form. This helps everyone get to know "their" gardener a bit. Things to include are level of gardener, type of gardener (cut flowers, veggies, herbs, etc.), favorite plants, other hobbies, favorite dish to cook, and so on. The more details you extract, the more personal the gifts become. Each participant then draws a name out of a hat and gets to know their assigned gardener via their About Me form. Everyone then gathers in a few weeks and exchanges their gifts. Not only does this make home gardening feel much more communal in the shared love of it, but rarely do adults get to delight in gifts so personal, heartfelt, and tailored just for you. I absolutely recommend this to kickstart spring or autumn and create merriment for a group.

The second approach to a seed swap is more literal and more traditional. It's a party where all the participants share their collections of seeds. This can include saved seeds, unopened seed packets, half-used seed packets, etc. You all get together to review and share seed stashes, offering tips on what did well, how the harvest went, what to look out for, and so on. In the end, everyone increases their personal seed bank. The idea here is that each year, with just a few extra seeds, you can save money and try new varieties of plants, in turn saving your own seeds from the yield. Bonus points if you all bring great recipes too!

WREATH-MAKING EVENT

A great kick-off to the holiday season—or the change of any season, really—is a wreath-making party. You can either pre-forage for the branches used to create the wreath bases, purchase them together as a group, or have guests bring their own. For a wreath party I hosted, we used thin and pliable olive branches with some red-berried native shrub branches twisted in for a Christmas-time gathering. Have available for each guest: ribbons, twine, floral wire, cinnamon sticks, bells, dried oranges, and dried flowers. Everyone gets to twist their own wreath, as well as adorn it however they choose.

GRUB DIG

For the little kids in your life, nothing is more enchanting than getting to have free reign in digging something up. After a horrible year of Japanese beetles, we were left with an obnoxious number of grubs. This called for an event where we invited a bunch of kids (and brave parents) who wanted to garden to come rip out our old plants, and then dig up the garden and search for grubs. Make it a competition if you'd like, honoring whoever finds the biggest grub, the most, the smallest, etc. Set out yummy garden snacks like carrots, celery with peanut butter and raisins, and all the healthy goodies kids normally shy away from. The garden tends to inspire even the pickiest eaters to try new things.

A GARDEN-RAISING

In Amish and other rural communities, when a new barn is built, there is a community barn-raising. All the able-bodied folks come together and physically erect the barn, raising its sides, assembling the final shape of the building, and placing it where it needs to rest. The act of many makes the task manageable. A new garden is a great opportunity to gather some friends to make the work lighter. The day of placing raised beds and filling them with soil is a great time to make a gathering of it. Everyone gets to help bring the garden to life, fill it up, and then eventually they get to come back for a harvest dinner.

Inviting friends into the garden is a gift to not just them, but also you.

HERBY BREAD BAKING

Something everyone can benefit from learning hands-on is bread baking. Whether you feel equipped to teach this or want to rely on YouTube, it doesn't matter. Gather a group of friends, have everyone bring a bag of flour, and then let them go out to the kitchen garden and pick some herbs. You can all bake a loaf of bread together and learn an age-old skill with a garden twist. If you're advanced and have sourdough starter, that's even better! If you're just wanting to make a fun artisan loaf with some yeast, that works beautifully, too. Getting to go pick some herbs from a garden, then coming inside and immediately putting them to use is so gratifying and unites us in a beautiful camaraderie around hard work and handcraft.

While there is the art of gathering veggies for harvests, there are so many ways to also gather with our people. So many of us work from home, locked into silos of our own creation and then seeking solitary scrolling activities to "break" from our busy day. No more, my friends, no more. The garden is designed to take you back to nature, allowing you to extend an invitation to those near and dear to you as well.

CHAPTER 7

CONNECT

When I was a child, I would spend lazy summer mornings running around the house in my jammies, typically one of my mother's t-shirts. I remember wandering out to the back of the property barefoot, crouching under the metal gate to get into the pasture, careful to give glaring and tough-looking side glances to the mules so they wouldn't bother me. I would then sneak under another gate into the unruly back part of our property. I can remember the blackberry hedges towering over me with their dark green, jagged leaves and menacing thorns, with the mysterious creek a few yards beyond. I carefully gathered the ripest berries I could reach without pushing into the rugged patch, and gently placed them in the bottom part of my mom's shirt I had pulled up to make a pouch. I crept home to show my parents my treasure. After a gentle "tsk tsk" for staining mom's shirt, we made cobbler from my berries. Man, *that* was living.

When in high school, I remember sneaking out to go to a party in an abandoned summer house in a town that flooded every winter. We canoed into the house and snuck up the stairs. *That* was living. And then in college, I'll never forget a week-long water-gun fight we had on campus with a frater-nity, dressed in black head to toe, nearly getting expelled when we got caught playing capture the flag as our final coup d'etat and it resulted in the flooding of the bottom floor of said fraternity. *That* was living. And then I remember returning home after completing all my schooling, finding a meadow filled with wildflowers and laying under a blanket of flawlessly oscillating stars with my fu-ture husband, feeling my smallness and largeness simultaneously. *That* was living.

The thread that I have found so gently sews all these seams together is connection—to others, to nature, to self. It's such a gorgeous rambling road we walk, and now in the prime of motherhood, there is the ultimate daily connection with my husband and children, pushing me into myself and into them, out into the garden, and back—all forms of connection that take a matter of minutes most days. We learn how to come close and then go far from what we value as we grow up, until one day we get to fold everything in together and live closely with all we hope to hold. In many ways, the kitchen garden calls us homeward. It allows us to discover the awe and wonder in each day, connect-ing us back to the place we often seek to find—a peaceful home within ourselves.

◄ A gift of the garden is that you think you're connecting to nature, when really you're connecting to yourself.

Connection in the garden starts with getting to know the soil and plants there, and then it blossoms as we uncover new varieties and new ways to prepare delicious meals from our harvest. I often wander into the garden with a basket in the crease of my elbow, not sure of what I'll find and thinking there's not much to take. I'll return with armfuls of treasure—perhaps four giant tufts of dill begging to be tzatziki, two handfuls of purple snap peas for fresh munching, a few calendula flowerheads to dry, and enough lettuce for everyone's lunch. Energy rushes through you as you allow the natural world to uplift and inspire you, and to return you to that creative place where you get to gratefully commune with nature and then go inside and make magic in the kitchen.

Inviting others into this moment is often what makes it most palpable. Sharing yourself with someone is the fastest way to intimacy, and it unlocks an authentic connection. In this chapter, we'll touch on that, along with ways to connect specifically with plants to enhance your knowledge and build your intuition.

Connecting with Plants

As we get to know new plants, we awaken an opportunity within ourselves. I find it is vitally important to listen to the call of what interests you as a starting point. What you're drawn to is your intuition pushing you, and perhaps a plant calling you in. Many herbalists will tell you plants can communicate (we know scientifically they have a level of awareness—just not as extensive as our own) and can often align with what you need, popping into your head at a particular time for a reason.

I see this with volunteer plants. A "volunteer" is a plant that grows randomly somewhere in the garden, and I believe they show up for a reason. They're serving you with some wisdom, either from what they can offer, or how you'll respond to their presence. At times I've found an abundance of the common weed crab grass popping up just in time for me to slow down and process something that's happening in my life—an exercise made abundantly easier while weeding. Busy

Taste, touch, smell, and work with plants to connect and get to know them.

hands make for a clear mind. I've found some volunteer tomatoes popping up in the most unusual and inhospitable environments during seasons when I needed the lycopene their fruits provide, which serves us in many ways, from improved cognitive function and bone health to the many other benefits antioxidants like it impart. For a more logical approach, we see plants like citrus ready to harvest during the cool season, just when we need their potent vitamin C and bright flavor to lift us through the darker months and help flavor heavier foods.

To begin to connect with what's already available, take a walk around your property and note what's present. Are dandelions taking over? Their roots are great medicine, their flowers can be made into wine, and their leaves are an edible, early-spring green. Perhaps you have a single blackberry bush that's been languishing or some bulbs that keep pushing up out of the ground. Are you meant to be cultivating these, learning from them, or working with them? An awareness of what you need as a person and what you can do in the garden as a co-creator with nature is the next level of connection with and beyond the garden.

To connect to yourself with each season, get to know the new plants and new varieties available during that time of year. Test the edges of your climate and plant things in ways you haven't tried. Go inward and see what *you* need. If you're in a busy season, perhaps it's time to try a cover crop like rye or clover in some beds and reap the powerful impact of resting the soil, which also offers rest to the gardener.

Finally, as you get to know each plant, get to know *all* parts of it and all of its uses. Like the dandelion or a rose, whose petals are fantastic when distilled into a fragrant water and whose hips (seed pods) are a great source of nutrients, most plants have many uses.

The next level of knowing a rose is knowing that a great companion for it is garlic. Garlic also has many parts and many uses. In addition to its edible bulb, if you're growing hardneck varieties,

---

A WORD ABOUT PLANT PARTS

Let's start with the **roots**, which, depending on the plant, are sometimes edible and enjoyed roasted, shaved, dried, or pureed. This plant part absorbs water and nutrients from the soil, as well as anchoring the plant to it. In many ways, roots are the strength of the plant.

Stems transport water, nutrients, hormones, and other soluble materials throughout the plant, and provide support to the leaves and flowers—pushing them toward the sun to promote growth and development.

The **leaves** make food for the plant—and, in some cases, for us too. They convert sunlight, carbon dioxide, and water into sugars and oxygen through photosynthesis.

The **flowers and petals** call in pollinators and other insects to come feed on their nectar and pollen. As they feed, the insects carry pollen to other plants, leading to the creation of fruits, vegetables, and eventually, seeds, which then carry on the lifecycle of the plant.

---

the scapes (flower stalks) are important to prune off and delicious to sauté or throw on the barbecue. Grapes are another multifaceted plant. The fruit is delicious raw or made into juice, and the leaves are great for dolmas and cheese trays. Fennel, too, is a plant worth knowing for its fantastic edible bulbous stem. But it also has feathery leaves for flavoring food and edible seeds that are a favorite ingredient in Italian regions. Once toasted, their woody licorice flavor is enhanced. Not to mention the many pollinators who source nectar from fennel flowers.

As you explore your garden, aim to become as vast in your knowledge as your curiosity allows. Seek to maximize each unique offering in as many ways as possible.

Smelling the fresh dill and nasturtium leaves as I harvest them for lunch.

THE GOAL

The analogies are endless when it comes to plants and humans—the circle of our lives, our rise and fall, can so naturally be seen in the short span of a flower being "born" and then fading away. Our journeys, though typically longer than that of a plant, are beautiful and useful throughout, much like our leafed friends. I was gifted the opportunity to be by my father's side as he passed away. I got to see the value and beauty of his life in its full arc. Much like when we let a cherished flower go to seed, gently allowing the full lifecycle to come to fruition and then carefully collecting the legacy of the plant into our pocket for future planting, people too fade away, leaving us with stories, recipes, notions, and perhaps the potential to keep growing. In the final moments of my father's life, we all gently stopped holding his hand, fussing over his blankets, caressing his arms, and chatting softly with him. In the hours prior, we shared our stories, gave final hugs, and wiped tears away as we gave and asked for forgiveness and read prayers. But when it was time—we just knew it was time—

we physically let go. And so did he. In the garden, letting go is easier, of course. Mostly because we have much less emotion, memory, and feeling tied to it all. But the process is quite the same.

Whether in the garden or in life, connection is the goal—to ourselves, to each other, and to nature, our great teacher. Observe it all with awe and as though it is magic (because it is). See your life at present expand, slow down, and become more fruitful. Go out and observe, honor the process, celebrate the successes, and know the failures are all by design.

Forging the Nature Connection with Children

By far one of the greatest joys of my life has been fostering in my children a love of nature and the garden. I was honestly terrified that being stuck in suburbia meant they'd live a sterile and contrived life. I had this yearning for them to live a life that builds character, resilience, and a genuine curiosity for the world. All the best people I knew growing up were deeply in touch with nature, and so I sought to create that for my kids as well.

I was not a dirt lover as a child, and I have always used a loose grip when guiding my children toward our garden, knowing they may never take to it like I did (admittedly at the age of thirty, so there's time!), but also knowing that if a seed is planted, the right circumstances will eventually bring it to life. Witnessing an adult in your life be in love with something typically sets a good example, and I am grateful to have found a love for gardening and cooking and the overall giving of myself wholeheartedly to a life I chose.

▶ Little ones are much more capable than we think. We teach tool safety very early on so that the children can help us and feel a sense of pride and responsibility.

My oldest son was by my side from the very start of my gardening endeavors, eating handfuls of dirt, exploring pill bugs, and munching on the green tops of my onion plants. He was enamored from the beginning. My daughter loves to complete tasks with me. She can be found picking nasturtium seeds off the vines, eager to complete the job and move onto the next, interfacing with the garden in her own way. Though less excited by the plants, she loves to be near mom, and that is always something I say yes to. I know how fleeting that season is. My youngest is still in the passive phase, gazing up to see a flock of birds travel the sky, enamored by the sight and sound of the wind tickling the trees. Babies love to be outside and there's truly no better place for them than tucked into a wrap on your chest while you deadhead flowers or pinch off squash blossoms for frying.

While being outside is paramount, and I adore the approach of letting our children learn to be bored, there are also a handful of tips and tricks I've employed when it comes to engaging our little ones with nature. After interviewing dozens of people about their own gardening experiences, I've discovered there is a common theme. As a child, there was an adult they admired or respected who introduced them to gardening and passed on the legacy. Whether it unlocked immediately or much later in life, there was an example set that baked the interest into them.

GARDENING WITH CHILDREN

There are four main approaches I take when it comes to gardening with children, and I find that categorizing them in my mind helps me to stay unattached to the outcome. However, I have found these approaches to be tried and true. My three kids are wildly different, but they all have a place in the garden. I also keep the kitchen garden a chore-free zone—pulling weeds being the only exception. They do outdoor chores, such as leaf raking, but I do not make the kitchen garden an obligation.

We let all carrots be "snackers" to be enjoyed while out in the garden.

The first approach begins the moment they're outside with you as a baby. One of the best things you can do for infants is narrate the world to them. I'll chat with babies about what I'm seeing and take their hands and introduce the sense of touch to them. "Smooth leaf," "rough bark," and so on. As children get older, this continues but they can interact independently with what interests them as you narrate. Eventually, once they start crawling and walking, they follow you out into the garden just to be near you. This stage is one of the most underrated, yet it showcases so clearly that whatever you are interested in, they're interested in—if only for a small window of time. Savor this time; it's fleeting.

The next phase is exploring garden and nature crafts and activities. Children learn through play, so attaching joy and curiosity to nature has been a primary goal for me with the kids. This felt especially important as I realized we were going to live in the suburbs for my children's childhoods. I remember being in a business meeting with some men I respected and telling them about how

I never wanted to raise my kids in Orange County, California, and I was so worried about the culture they'd be exposed to. "You raise your kids in your own backyard," they told me. It was the truth I needed to hear. The place is less important than the presence, and even in the depths of a city or suburb we can seek out the wild world for a hike, a nature scavenger hunt, or a rooftop garden.

The key to nature activities is to allow for the awe and magic to come in. Let them explore, be hands on, and use all their senses. We do digs, seek and finds, hidden toy hunts, leaf rubs, wildflower-ball making, and so much more. As they get older, engaging kids when they would otherwise be uninterested looks a lot like asking questions or making statements like, "I put something new in the garden called a Bug Snug. Let me know when you find it," and off they go, casually acting as though they maybe don't even care, until they find the thing and start asking questions. I especially love sending friends with adolescent kids out into the garden to harvest with very vague descriptions and letting the pre-teens run wild discovering the joy of picking peas and being a no-fail beginner. Once they find the fairy door, the world opens to them.

The third way I like to engage little ones is by giving them age-appropriate jobs. The sweet spot for children gardening is about four to ten. This is when they're most eager and can really help you. There are myriad jobs to be done, and the younger they are, the more you break a task up into tiny doable pieces. Digging holes for transplanting veggies? Let your two-year-old hold a kid-sized shovel and watch, or just push the dirt around. By the age of three, they're digging. By four, the hole is the right size and they're putting the plant in, backfilling, and watering. Tasks can be as small as holding things or catching bugs and as big as sowing seeds and harvesting dinner.

Last, allowing children to have their own garden space is the real cherry on top. Let them fully choose what to plant, when, and how. Let them come up with a watering schedule or go on

> ## 10 GREAT GARDEN JOBS FOR KIDS
>
> 1. Digging holes with a small spade
> 2. Placing plants in holes
> 3. Pulling plants out of trays
> 4. Catching bugs
> 5. Removing pests
> 6. Deadheading flowers
> 7. Saving seeds
> 8. Sowing seeds
> 9. Watering
> 10. Harvesting

instinct. You'll have to guide the process based on how your family personalities are, but this is really where the magic happens. Some kids feel very called to care for their piece of the garden with longevity and some lose interest quickly. Small interest? Maybe work on a small potted garden. Big interest? Maybe give them half of a raised bed. Allowing the process to unfold can be maddening, but for kids, it's a safe space to play and learn (for us too!).

The apocalyptic year of 2020 was when we really honed our garden activities. Quarantined for months as a nation was shocking and even fatal for many, but for others, it was freeing and lovely. I had one of the best years of my life, leaning into the at-homeness of it all, cultivating an in-ground garden, keeping my then eight-month-old and two-year-old busy as a stay-at-home mom. I really liked how the pressure to do and go and be dissolved, and we instead found ourselves back in time, like homesteaders from a century past, separated from distant family and pushed to self-reliance. During this time, we played, we explored, and we lived well as a unit, learning together.

10 GARDEN AND NATURE ACTIVITIES FOR THE FAMILY

1. Make Wildflower Balls

These are also called *seed bombs*, but that feels a bit aggressive to me. To make them, gather up some clay—we used our native soil (it's *that* claylike)—or buy clay at a craft store (not air-dry clay, just normal molding clay). Dampen the clay and then mix in native wildflower seeds, forming balls as you go. Once the damp clay and seed balls are formed, let them dry overnight. The next day, head out and throw your wildflower balls into nature, plopping the seeds wherever you go!

2. Make Seed Paper

Recycled paper is so fun and easy to make. Adding seeds is the ultimate up-level. To a blender, add some torn up recyclable paper and warm water. Ideally, fill half the blender with torn paper and then fill it to the top with warm water. Blend until a mushy pulp forms. While the pulp is still in the blender, add wildflower seeds and mix it with a spoon—don't blend! Lay the seed-infused mush out onto a strainer (we use a round, flat-mesh pan cover) to get as much water out as you can. Then lay out a dish cloth and spread the pulp onto that. Use a dry sponge to spread the pulp out and draw up even more water. Press the pulp into a thin layer, let it dry, and voila, you have seed paper that can be made into cards, written on, or just planted!

3. Flower Weavings

These are great for little ones who can't do much more than wander around and pick flowers. We've made many variations of this, and you can even make a large version with two sticks pushed into the dirt and some string. We enjoy a hand-held weaving made with a piece of cardboard (like a flap from a delivery box) with twine wrapped around it to create a taunt web of strings or a few tight string lines wrapped flat against the cardboard. Go out and pick flowers, adding them to your cardboard "tray" by tucking them under and

A scavenger hunt in the garden keeps kids occupied while mom gets work done.

over the strings to hold in the flowers. You'll end up with a woven pattern or a little flat bouquet, depending on how you wrap your twine.

4. Nature Scavenger Hunt

Scavenger hunts are a great way to buy yourself some time or to make up a game in nature when you have nothing with you. With young children, it's best to collect items from nature first and assemble them in a dish for them to then go find. As the kids get older, write out a list or draw pictures of what they need to find. The goal is to let them roam and see if they can gather or identify the items you've listed. You can also hide things in the garden for them to find, allowing your time together to be fun and productive.

5. Pinecone Birdseed Feeders

A quick and easy project, these little birdfeeders are fun because you can go foraging for the pinecones first, making it a multi-step adventure. Once you collect the pinecones, hot glue a piece of twine onto the pointy end to hang them up with later. Once the glue is dry, slather the pinecone with peanut butter, spreading it on all the little brackets of the cone. Last, roll your peanut butter–coated pinecone in birdseed or dump it on top—whichever mess you prefer to clean up. Then hang it on a tree and watch as the birds come calling.

6. Start Seeds in an Egg Carton

Children love to take trash and make it into a treasure. Egg cartons give that upcycled charm and are so functional. I recommend using recyclable cardboard cartons. Once you've eaten the eggs, cut the bottom half of the carton from the top. The top flap will become a tray for any water that seeps through. Fill the bottom flap with soil in each egg compartment. Sprinkle a seed into each compartment, choosing seeds that only need to be covered by ¼ inch (0.6 cm) of soil. Sprinkle a light layer of soil on top of the seeds and water daily. Place the newly planted tray in a sunny window with the top flap underneath it to catch any extra water seepage.

7. Dino Dig

Pull this project out when you're having one of those days. All you need is a bucket of dirt and some tiny plastic or wooden toys. We used little plastic dinosaurs left over from a birthday party goody bag. Bury the toys in the bucket of dirt and then give your kids a shovel. Tell them how many items are buried and watch them explode with excitement every time they uncover a new find.

8. Flower Crowns

This is an ageless activity! Go out and find some pliable branches—about two or three, each long enough to make its way around your kid's head. Wrap them together like a twist tie, overlapping the ends until you have a circular crown. Then weave flowers into the twisted branches. You can also create a flower crown with just flowers by taking one flower with a long stem and adding stems to it using the same twisting motion. Every few inches, add a new stem into the twisting mix. Eventually each flower stem gets twisted among at least two others and you have a flower crown without branches.

A bug snug hiding in the corner of the garden.

9. DIY Bug Snug

A bug snug is a little stack or teepee made from garden debris and sticks, left out in the garden for the bugs to find and overwinter in. They can be made any time of year, though I recommend the start of the cool season because that's when pollinators need homes. Have the kids find big sticks to make the frame of the teepee and then small sticks and other debris to fill it up. Keep adding to it over time, making this an ongoing task for little ones.

10. Garden Counting

This may seem rudimentary, but in the dog days of motherhood it's simple and easy—like a game of "I spy." Ask your child to go find six pink flowers, or two green leaves, or see how many pumpkin sprouts they can count. It not only is teaching them counting and colors, but it's also acquainting them with the plants and helping them to identify them by name. These tiny games make the garden so much easier to access and so familiar.

Natural lessons occur moment by moment when the kids are involved.

There are endless ways to engage kids outside, but the act of being helpful in and of itself builds their confidence and proves to be wildly useful as they age. It may seem small, but having your four-year-old run out and know how to properly identify and harvest parsley is such a gift and something that certainly is not taught in a conventional school. The connection goes beyond child and nature and forges a bond between child and caregiver. To have the garden in common, to invite little ones in, and to make it their place, too—that is a forever gift.

Kitchen Garden Generosity

There is a level of hospitality—or perhaps generosity—all kitchen gardeners have. If I were a betting woman, I'd bet that anyone you bump into who also has an abundant garden would invite you in for coffee or pick up the tab at lunch. It reminds me of growing up in a small town. My mom is the most generous woman I've ever met and anytime someone stopped by the house, whether it was an electrician, the veterinarian, or the "naked lady"

neighbor who used to mow her lawn in the nude, my mother would offer them a beverage and ask if they wanted to stay for dinner. She impressed this upon me, making it a custom my husband and I now teach our children. It's a general principle of hospitality, but it's also something that strengthens the culture of your home. Life in the garden leaves us even better able to share and connect with people in a way that goes beyond a gesture. This is sharing the bounty, giving a piece of your heart and hard work. The current generation of adults is just on the fringe of being able to remember when times were simpler, when there was no internet and recipes were handed down or torn from magazines. We just narrowly snuck a peek at that life, earning a level of nostalgia for a time when it was still in good form to cook from scratch or bake cookies for a new family at school. I have found that inspiration abounds in the food garden and that sharing from it really binds us closer to those around us. People are inherently looking to belong, and nothing says, "you belong" like a big ol' armful of homegrown veggies or some potato kale soup from your backyard.

Connecting with your garden's harvest is the first step in a desire to share with others. The rest of this chapter tackles some ideas for what to do with all the goodness, aside from the common cooking and eating we all know and love. There are many ways to cook, eat, preserve, and overall enjoy the aftermath of all your hard work in the garden. Staying organized and motivated is half the battle in figuring out what to do with the harvest. We'll also review some basics to consider when it comes to being a good steward of your garden's yield.

PANTRY STAPLES FOR YOURSELF AND TO SHARE

The secret ingredient in so many meals in my home are things like chive salt or homegrown tomatoes I froze and processed for later use. You don't have to be a full-on homesteading, canning, off-the-grid maverick to be inserting beauty from your garden into everyday meals. Simply allow the harvest to inform your meals and then implement some tricks your future self will thank you for later. Here are a few of my own pantry staples you can start adding to your home stock immediately and through the many coming growing seasons.

Herbed Salts

This is the silent hero of most meals in my home. Chive salt was my foray into herbed salts and now I sprinkle a touch of this into most savory meals like it's my own personal pixie dust. Similar to the onion or garlic salt you buy, herbed salts add flavor and dimension, but more subtly. There is still a place for granulated garlic and other spices, but these herbed salts are often what I use instead of plain-old kosher salt. Feel free to replace the chives with dill, rosemary, basil, parsley, or whatever you'd like.

Ingredients:
- ½ cup (24 g) chives
- 1 cup (300 g) kosher salt

Method:
Heat oven to 200°F (93°C). Gather chives and lightly rinse and pat them mostly dry. Add the chives to the salt and place them into a food processor or blender. A mortar and pestle will do, too, but it takes longer (like most good things!). Blend until just combined, then spread the salt mixture onto a cookie sheet. Bake at a low heat for about 15 to 25 minutes, turning the salt every 10 minutes or so, so nothing burns or actually cooks. You want the herbs to dry out and infuse the salt, but not cook or burn.

Let the salt cool and then store in an airtight glass container for use throughout year. Small jars of herbed salts make a great hostess or teacher gift too!

Note: The proportions can easily be increased by following the basic ratio of ½ cup (24 g) herbs to 1 cup (300 g) salt.

Blending up a fresh batch of chive salt.

Laminated pasta with primrose flowers.

Dried Flower and Herb Pasta

Pasta is simply better when handmade. Layering herbs and flowers into the pasta really takes things up a notch and it is so easy. The method I like the most is lamination. Here's how to do it.

Ingredients:

- 2 cups (232 g) 00 Flour (all-purpose flour works too)
- 3 eggs + 1 egg yolk
- 1 tablespoon (15 ml) olive oil
- Handful edible flowers or herbs (pansies, primrose, parsley, oregano, nasturtium all work well)

Method:

To make the pasta, create a mound with the flour and then push a dent into the center that is deep but with high walls—this is your "well." Drop the eggs into the well of flour and begin to gently stir them with a fork, pulling some flour into the well. This eventually combines your eggs and flour. If you feel shaky about the endeavor, put your flour and eggs in a bowl instead of loose on the counter (we don't need to tell the Italians about this). Once the dough starts to form and gets shaggy, get in there with your hands and start kneading. If it stays really sticky, add more flour. If it's not becoming a solid dough (similar to a modeling clay texture), add olive oil or a splash of water.

Once you have a ball of dough, cover and let rest for about 30 minutes. Don't skip this step.

Once rested, cut the ball into four pieces. Flatten each piece into the shape of a long lasagna noodle, which you can later shape into whatever pasta you'd like. To flatten, if using a pasta maker or attachment to a mixer, first shape your dough into a long rectangle and flatten a bit with your palm so it can feed into your pasta maker. Keep tightening your pasta maker with each pass until the dough is long and thin. If you're rolling out by hand, the shape doesn't matter as much, but I still recommend a rectangle so you can easily laminate in the flowers. To flatten by hand, use a rolling pin

and just keep rolling until your shoulders want to break off and the pasta is very thin.

Once you have your dough thinned, it should also be long. Bring the top of the dough piece to the bottom to see where the middle point is and then cut it in half so that you have two pieces of the same length. Lay one piece down, and then place your edible flowers and/or herbs onto that. If your flowers still have the green pedicel attached, remove that so there aren't big bumps in your pasta. Take the second sheet of dough and gently place it on top of the flowers. You'll then have one new piece of pasta dough that you'll flatten again either with your pasta maker or with a rolling pin. You may need to do this step a couple of times to really get those flowers laminated into the dough.

Now, you have flower pasta! From here, cut the pasta and make it a shape like fettuccine, or keep the sheets wide and long for lasagna. To dry the pasta, hang them up on something like a pasta drying rack or the back of a chair. For cooking, place them in boiling and salted water for about three minutes, or until the pasta starts to float. Pasta cooks very fast when fresh.

Easy Chicken Stock

A fantastic way to use all your garden veggie scraps and herbs is to use them in stocks and broths. I do this by keeping a freezer bag in the freezer to collect all my veggie trimmings, onion skins, garlic ends, etc., adding to it each time I cook until it's full. Once I have enough scraps gathered, I use them to make a veggie broth, bone broth, or this chicken stock.

Ingredients:
- Whole chicken carcass
- 1 freezer bag's worth of veggie scraps
- Water

Method:
To make a chicken stock, collect the bones from a whole chicken—a little meat left on the bone is fine—and combine those with a bag of frozen veggie scraps in a large stock pot. Cover the ingredients with enough water to fully submerge everything and bring it to a boil. Once at a boil, reduce the heat to a simmer and let it simmer for a couple of hours, then cool on the stove. Strain out the bones and veggie scraps. Pour the broth into jars and can them with a pressure canner, or pour the broth into freezer bags or molds to freeze. I use something called "souper cubes," which are pre-portioned silicone trays that allow you to freeze 2-cup (475-ml) measurements of broth for exact portioning.

Frozen homemade chicken stock is a lifesaver and staple in our kitchen.

Note: there will be gelatinous fat in your stock—that's good! It's full of nutrients. Also, when you're deciding how much water to use, you're also committing to how much storage space you have and how watery, or rich, the flavor of your broth is.

Classic Marinara

Oh, marinara, how you make me swoon! I grow tomatoes specifically for this reason (and to enjoy tomato sandwiches that are equal parts mayonnaise, cheddar, bread, and tomato).

The thing about marinara is that it's just so dang easy—it's dinner insurance! Bad day? Spaghetti. Rushed? Spaghetti. Kids are staging a coup? Spaghetti. Feeling ambitious and nostalgic? Shakshuka (a Middle Eastern dish with cooked eggs in a tomato base like your marinara for a savory and showy breakfast).

This marinara recipe is loose, but it's based off about 2 pounds (907 g) of tomatoes—you can't go wrong, just trust your instincts, and adjust quantities accordingly.

Ingredients:
- 2 pounds (907 g) tomatoes
- 8 garlic cloves, minced or pressed
- 4 onions, chopped
- Salt to taste
- Generous bunches of fresh parsley, basil, and oregano

Method:
Gather as many tomatoes as you can, chop them, and place in a baking dish (or many baking dishes if you have a lot of tomatoes). Add a bit of salt and roast the tomatoes in a 375°F (190°C) oven until soupy. This should take about an hour. Alternatively, you can roast them in a low barbecue for a few hours. Stir the tomatoes as you go, checking on them every 30 minutes or so. You want the tomatoes to split and be really loose but not have charred skin.

Once roasted, run the tomatoes through a juicer or food mill (a juicing attachment for a mixer works too) to remove the skins and seeds because they create bitterness. Warm the puree over the stove with the chopped onions, minced garlic, fresh basil, parsley, and oregano. Cook until the onions are soft. You can then either eat the marinara immediately or can or freeze it for later consumption.

Note: Taking the seeds out of the tomatoes is crucial. The seeds will make your sauce bitter, so don't skip this step.

The Quick Pickle

This is also called a refrigerator pickle and can be made in minutes but lasts weeks. Quick pickling avoids all the canning gear and still achieves a great pickle taste. You can use this method with most vegetables as well, in the event you'd like pickled carrots or radishes.

Ingredients:

- 2 cups (475 ml) water
- 1 cup (235 ml) vinegar
- 2 teaspoons (9 g) sugar
- 1 large cucumber
- 2 garlic cloves, cut in half
- 2 teaspoons (2.6 g) dill
- Salt
- Pepper

Method:

1. Put water, vinegar, and sugar into a saucepan over medium heat. Stir until dissolved (about 3 minutes) to make a brine.
2. Let sit and cool off the burner for about 5 minutes.
3. Cut your cucumber into spears, and place into jar with garlic, dill, salt and pepper.
4. Pour brine into jar.
5. Let jar reach room temperature on the counter.
6. Refrigerate overnight before enjoying.

FOR THE LITTLE ONES

It's messy, but children love to pour. Let them pour the brine into the pickles and even stuff the cucumbers into the jars. Encourage them to pick all the herbs for these and other recipes (while working on their plant skills) and help twist on jar lids. Some seasons the kids are willing, but not yet able. In those instances, have them hand you things or sit at the counter while you work and keep you company.

It's quite an American phenomenon to be so disconnected from where our food comes from; we've outsourced so much growing. With convenience comes the loss of many skills. Many countries around the world still have a vibrant farmer's market system or it's more common to tend a little home garden, both of which keep the human-food connection alive. With each year's kitchen garden, you're nurturing a better relationship between food and people—reminding all of how true nourishment comes to the plate.

CHAPTER 8

INSPIRE

With our very first property, I didn't have the space or sunlight to grow anything in our side yard. There was some communal land right in front of our townhouse that looked like it was our land but was managed by the homeowners association (HOA). It was just some lawn that was in bad shape due to the water restrictions placed on multi-unit housing developments because of the drought in California. We had to petition our HOA to use the space for a kitchen garden, and my husband had the wonderful idea of making it a community garden of sorts. I planned and prepared a presentation, complete with photos and answers to any predicted concerns. I had done water research and was even willing to use our personal water supply for the garden (which I eventually did by dragging a 100-foot [30.5-m] hose through our house every day). To try and sweeten the deal for everyone involved, I offered to let others share the growing space or I would share whatever I grew with everyone.

To be honest, in the beginning, I didn't want to share anything, but the idea grew on me, and I knew it was a fair offer. The members of the HOA and individual homeowners didn't show much interest, but they liked the idea of the garden and thought it would be a bit prettier than their plan of putting a bench and some plain stones there. So, they gave me license to plant whatever I wanted. No one wanted to garden, so that part was all up to me.

I ran with my newfound freedom and went on to build two raised beds surrounded by river rocks with some stepping stones in between. I planted out warm-season plants and waited for the magic to happen.

That first season I only really remember one thing. On the day our basil was ready, I was having horrible stomach cramps. Though I knew intuitively what was happening, I was determined to harvest that basil and bundle it up sweetly for the neighbors. I had an abundance of it and was so excited to make good on my promise. I had bought some gift tags to attach to the tied-up bundles of basil. I harvested everything carefully and used twine to make the gathered stems really look cute. I laid them out in a basket and took my one-year-old son with me door to door to deliver the bundles. People were so delighted! They loved how fragrant the basil was and they wanted to know how to use it—most had never tasted homegrown basil. They also asked about the other vegetables I was growing.

◀ Garden bundles for neighbors are always a good idea.

I, in turn, was so inspired by the exchanges that it fueled my love of gardening even more. Getting to share what I grew and talk about the garden really connected us, and it became a sweet activity to do with my son. The whole endeavor gave me a purpose I hadn't anticipated. The day of that very first harvest was one I was so proud of, but it was also one I was deeply saddened by. Delivering the basil bundles was a welcome distraction from losing the baby we were expecting but hadn't yet told the world about. The duality of the experience stuck with me, but it also continues to be one I hold dear to my heart for the way it kept me going through an unbearably painful time. It was the first of many life events to unfold at the edge of my garden beds. Enduring hardships in life unites us to both people and ourselves in ways we'd sometimes rather avoid, though being human means we cannot. As gardeners, we have the privilege of a space to process and spend time in nature to heal and connect. Out in the wild, everything makes a bit more sense, even the difficult parts.

From that day forward, the neighbors came to expect my garden bundles. I would harvest whatever was ready, perhaps a bunch of lettuce, green onions, some marigolds, and spinach, and I would wrap them all up in brown paper, tying it together with a jute string. These bundles were adorable and entirely fun to make. The joy in collecting the harvest, laying it all out, wrapping it up, and then summoning my son to deliver them with me was second-to-none on my list of fulfilling activities. Likewise, the neighbors became more and more inspired to come look at the garden, try new foods and recipes, and get to know us and their food better. Deep in the heart of suburbia, where every convenience reigns supreme and there's a Starbucks on almost every corner, neighborly generosity and self-reliance skills were showing themselves to still be valuable.

Delivering some of our very first garden bundles to neighbors.

I do believe a part of the calling of the kitchen garden is for its yield to be shared. The beauty of the space you design will beckon on-lookers, but the brawn and utility of it have the potential to inspire people to follow new paths. The famous quote is, "A rising tide lifts all ships," but I like to think of it as "A growing garden saves all souls." That's why children are so attracted to gardening—it unlocks wonder and awe. To share your kitchen garden experience is to share joy. In this chapter, we'll explore ways to do this, with the goal of continuing to inspire others and keep the next generation in the garden.

Garden Bundles

To make your own garden bundles, I recommend keeping a few items on hand: brown construction or kraft paper, twine, and some plastic bags or reusable snack bags. Harvest from the garden whatever is ready, always trying to include some herbs and flowers, too. Lay everything out and rinse it off, if needed. Once it's laid out and you can clearly see everything you've harvested, break each crop into little groups based on your yield. Then start to build your bundles by creating small piles with the tallest vegetables on the bottom and the smallest on top. For example, layer swiss chard in first, then some arugula, then some thyme, and then some fava beans. Then dampen a paper towel or hand towel to wrap around the base of any cut stems—just the leafy greens in this instance, to keep them from wilting and going bad. Place the towel-wrapped bottom of the plants into the plastic bag to retain the moisture. Next, wrap the whole bundle up in the brown paper, much like a florist would wrap a bouquet, trimming the paper to be about half the height of the arrangement and then folding each side of the paper diagonally over the bundle. Fold the bottom up as the final move, then fasten it all together with twine and voila! A stunning and rustic little vegetable parcel for sharing.

Wrap some fresh veggies in brown kraft paper, add some twine, and surprise a friend.

FOR THE LITTLE ONES

Children love being a part of gifting the bundles, accompanied by a caregiver, of course. We sometimes include little notes or recipes, and love to "ding-dong ditch" by ringing the doorbell, leaving the bundle, and then running away giggling, knowing we've gifted a fun surprise for whoever opens the door.

A Community Take-What-You-Need

The next level up from sharing garden bundles would be to create a little farmstand or a take-what-you-need crop share. These have been popping up more and more as the interest in gardening rises. It can be so rewarding to see how the community revels in free veggies! If there isn't enough of your own extra harvest to do this, consider teaming up with a few neighbors or friends who often have excess produce from their own gardens and coordinate a weekly day for stocking the farmstand. All you really need is a shaded and elevated shelf or cart for displaying the goodies, with some signage to indicate what everything is. I've seen bus stop shelters and even old refrigerators converted into little community share stands. Slap some chalk paint containers into a few pieces of wood and glue those on for labeling the offerings and you're off to the races! What I enjoy about this is the instant lift the community gets. Everyone is now endeared and intrigued. They're touched by the generosity and called to be their own highest selves, perhaps sharing their own surplus to contribute to the cause.

Teaching Others to Garden

I've said it once (or maybe a bajillion times?) and I'll say it again: Gardening changed my life. And I hope yours, too! At some point, if it wasn't a part of your upbringing, there was probably someone who inspired you to learn how to garden or at least expanded your idea of what is possible and worthwhile. My hope is to endow you with some tips for being *that* person for someone else, helping to keep the momentum going for this age-old practice of tending the earth and, really, tending ourselves. People are so intrigued, and yet often hesitant, to really dig into something new. They're worried about how much time it will take or who they'll become once this kind of shift in their lives has happened. You'll be the perfect guide for whomever approaches you and shows interest. Often, it's parents whose children are in love with the garden and can couch their interest as wanting to do something for their kids. That's fine—use the children to help you do the good stuff. I applaud it.

Here is some guidance for sharing your garden love and wisdom with others:

INVITE PEOPLE INTO YOUR GARDEN

It can feel cumbersome or awkward to be a kitchen garden missionary, but that's what you are now. When people show interest, invite them over. As adults, we so often forget that others want to be included and can feel easily intimidated by a new skill. Bring people to your garden, share what you're growing, offer true insight into what has worked for you and what has gone wrong, as well as how you overcame challenges. Offer to help friends think through their own space, and know that there are more people than you think who really want to get started but just don't know where to begin.

TINY HERB GARDENS

The most entry-level group of plants are herbs. They're easy to care for and take up little space. Gifting someone with a tiny herb garden—even one pot with one plant in it—is a gentle gesture that can really be useful and beautiful. Take it up a notch and consider a pot with an odd number of plants, say three or five, as it's most visually appealing. Try creating a theme for the herb planter, like Herbes de Provence with thyme, rosemary, tarragon, oregano, and basil, or a Greek theme with Greek oregano, mint, dill, fennel, and parsley. Be sure to add plant markers and choose a planter with drainage holes. Stock the planter with a good organic potting soil and consider adding a little card with care instructions.

Assemble your one-pot veggie garden with height and also root depth in mind.

ONE-POT VEGGIE GARDENS

People are often quite intimidated to start gardening, especially in small spaces, wondering if there's even anything they can do with just a patio or a rental with a small yard. The answer is, *yes*, always yes. I've found it to be awe inspiring to create a one-pot garden full of delightful vegetables and flowers. It works as either a gift or an activity when someone wants to learn how to garden and needs a very, very simple first nudge. The trick to a one-pot veggie garden is in following the basic structure of any decorative planter that will mature. You want a thriller, filler, and spiller to make the pot really shine with intentionality. The thriller is the tallest and biggest plant, the filler is a bushy plant that takes up the middle space, and a spiller drips over the edge. For example, it may be a pot with a swiss chard plant in the back, which gets quite tall and big, then chives and spinach in front of the chard, with some pansies to fill the middle space. The final touch would be strawberries planted near the edge so the berries can spill over as they grow.

There can be so many variations on this, but the ideal plants to go into a small planter are those with shallow roots that don't spread too much. Leafy greens are fantastic, and garlic is a great choice, as are pea plants growing up a small trellis, edible flowers, and of course, herbs.

HOSTING A GARDENING WORKSHOP

Gardening workshops are appealing to even experienced gardeners because we always want to know what others are doing—snagging secret tricks along the way. For new gardeners, it's helpful for making decisions, removing the overwhelm of too many options and allowing the focus to be on the lesson. I recommend hosting somewhere between three and fifteen people and having a theme for the workshop. Something like making the aforementioned herb container or one-pot garden is a good option. You provide the plants, soil, amendments, plant markers, and containers (or have it be "bring your own pot"), and give everyone a worksheet and plant info. It's a great way to teach people how to garden with a small project they get to "make and take." Leaving with something that goes home with them makes it a lasting lesson. Other possible themes are assembling a pizza garden (tomatoes, basil, oregano, peppers) or a salsa garden (tomatoes, onions, jalapeños, cilantro).

I've hosted fantastic workshops in partnership with a local boutique and restaurant. You bring the knowledge and the gardening goodies, and they provide the food and entertainment. Joining forces in the local community makes it so fun, but of course you can host at home as well and make an evening out of it.

CREATE A SCHOOL GARDEN

Many schools either would love a garden or have one that needs leadership after a passionate parent has moved on to a new school. School gardens are not so different than home gardens, except we really want to choose plants that are exciting to children and easy to care for. Some of the plants I recommend are strawberries because they're so pretty and tasty; radishes because they germinate quickly; rainbow chard for color; cherry tomatoes for fun and taste (kids are more apt to try something they grew and super-sweet varieties will delight them); edible flowers for fun; lettuce for easy salads kids can make; and squash, because they're so prolific and fun to watch grow quickly. Cucumbers are another win, as most kids enjoy eating them raw. In the school garden, kids can paint rocks and write the plant names on them, placing them next to the plant. They can water with watering cans, and they can, of course, learn about bugs, worms, butterflies, and other living creatures in the garden. Many local garden centers and nurseries are willing to donate soil and plants, and even gloves, so don't hesitate to reach out and partner with them.

Build a Seed Library

While some book libraries may include seed libraries, there are also independent tiny seed libraries popping up everywhere. The concept is like little free book libraries people build at parks or outside their home; "take a book/leave a book" being the basic principle. But instead of books, in seed libraries, people share seed packets by saving seeds from their gardens or getting donations from nurseries and seed companies to add to their little seed library boxes. Tiny seed libraries are usually built on the top of a 4 × 4-inch (10 × 10-cm) post, around the height of a mailbox. The library itself is a wooden box with a door that opens and a glass or plastic window so you can see inside. They typically have shelves with the seed packets stacked and organized inside. It's all hosted on an honor system, and many promote the use of local heirloom seeds.

Inspiring Others

There are many people mentioned in this book from my own upbringing and life, some of whom may never even know they're mentioned or the impact they made on me. That is the sparkle of inspiration capable of enriching people's lives, often unbeknownst to the giver of said inspiration. Perhaps you feel the impression you're making and want to rise to the occasion, or perhaps you don't and are just trying to provide inspiration because it makes you feel good. The dedication to the pursuit of gardening by those around me embedded in me so many things beyond the skill of growing food. It's a way of being—the connectedness to yourself and to nature and the commitment to carrying that connection into all relationships. It's the confidence to own that. It's the humility and bowing down to that which we cannot control and letting that be okay. It's the deep resolve to co-create, not for yourself, but for the future trees you will never sit beneath, but your children and grandchildren will. It's knowing that the calling, too, is vast and important and pushing aside the trivial and shortsighted in favor of the long-term. It reminds me of a piece of artwork by Kai Skye: "*I want to do important work, I said. Then smile at people you meet, she said & play with dogs & tuck a blanket around someone who falls asleep. That's not what I meant, I said. Of course you did, she said. You just had a small idea of important.*"

In modern days, many people may view the act of kitchen gardening as quite small, insignificant, or superfluous, perhaps. I assure you it is not. It is a great heroic act that keeps us sane, fed, satisfied, and tied to many things that deeply matter. Never underestimate the impact that living your absolute most true life and sharing that life with others will have. After interviewing dozens and dozens of gardeners on my podcast, I can say that their lives were all changed by the example of *one* person who shared their affection for gardening. It all manifests in different ways, with different preferences and styles, but the exposure to that person's affection bakes in an appreciation and spreads it, indelibly marking the hearts of those around them. And now, of those around *you*. That is the power of sharing your love of the garden with others.

▶ The next generation is worth gardening for.

Conclusion

As I was writing this book, I kept thinking to myself, "I can't forget to talk about . . . " and then I would jot down a note about something whimsical and non-practical, and then try to find a spot where it would make sense amidst the practical and functional knowledge. What I felt, and still feel, so desperate to convey was the non-essential component of kitchen gardening. It's the joy found in the complete admiration of a tulip with cream-striped, crimson petals, sprouting up from a bulb *you* kept in the fridge before planting, placing it just so in the soil and then returning with anticipation to heart-breakingly snip the bloom for a table vase, simultaneously proud and sad to remove it from its peaceful place. It's the way you find yourself again and again in awe of seeds sprouting and fruit forming, and the bees who came to the garden, and the birds bathing right in front of your eyes. It's the perfect, gentle curl of the pea tendril tips casually cascading their pods *down* while climbing in an imperceptible waltz *up* an iron trellis. It's the growing of cucamelons, just because you feel like it, and the tiny fractions of minutes spent observing the clouds move on their invisible tracks above, pressing pause on your worries for a moment, with a warm breeze hugging you as you wipe your hair back like a mother using her thumbs to wipe tears from her child's face.

There is an indescribable depth of satisfaction, joy, and comfort in tending to living things, in growing your food, in coaxing a flower from its seed. I hope you get to feel this and cling to its beauty as I have. There are many ways to garden, many philosophies and techniques—and, of course, many "experts." But there are just as many situations where it does not matter what you do because the bok choi will grow in the cold, hard clay despite your doubts. If it is meant to be so, it will be so. The garden humbles us in this way, like life often does.

I have now equipped you with enough information to seize all of the yummy potential in those green thumbs. We have designed, built, filled, and grown a garden together. We've got the knowledge to tend, and then take inside that which we harvest. We can store things, update the pantry, arrange the flowers we so lovingly planted for the bees and the tabletops, and we can even share what we know with the world, one child and one neighbor at a time. We are living inspired by the garden.

Most of the garden skill-building happens in the "growing" and "tending" sections that gardeners revisit each season, but each new year, it's fun to revisit your garden's design and see if you can add some character. Many garden builds can be multi-phase, with parts of the garden sitting unfinished until you have more time or more funding. New trellises are fun to build and move around; eventually you may add trees and shrubs; and often you may find you need to rethink things like the chosen pathway material or the amount of border you thought you wanted.

I find the difference between a novice gardener and the "expert" lies not in how well they are equipped or some inherent green thumbness (we know that doesn't exist), but in the questions they know to ask. No expert will ever know your garden quite like you do, especially after a few seasons, so keep that in mind. To move into a zone of greater

gardening genius, you have to know how to ask better questions.

If you feel stumped when it comes to garden design, ask yourself (or someone else), "What layers should I add? Does it feel the way I want it to feel?" If not, add some character or personal flair—perhaps a sculpture or a handmade trellis. If you're lost on what to grow, ask, "What do I enjoy eating? What does well in my hardiness zone? What troubles have I encountered that I now want to avoid?" The more you ask questions and get your hands dirty, the more you can harness useful curiosity as an ally.

I've covered where to place the garden, and how to get the soil going and the seeds growing. You now have lists of ways to tend and tinker and then venture into incorporating the garden into your everyday rhythms and recipes. Moving into the house, don't ask what makes a home, but rather ask, "What engages the senses? What delights? What celebrates the current season? What anchors us to our values and tethers us to the available gifts from the land?" Now these are some questions!

With all the ways to do the act of kitchen gardening, you are left to both self-explore, and of course, to get practical and start doing. The gentle doing of it all is what really presses the wrinkles out of it.

I often wonder if the ways of decades past will be moved forward, dated endlessly as "seventeenth century" or "that's so nineties," but being held dearly nonetheless. Kitchen gardening feels like this to me. Like a nod to the generations who *needed* a plot of their own to survive and reclaim their freedom, and who now inspire an edit to our own paths when we choose to take the slow, winding road back to a place where "made by hand" meant something. It is both a big and esoteric act and a quite small and banal one—so ordinary in so many ways—mattering so very much while just being something people do on the weekends.

We don't need scientific studies to tell us (although they have) that eating at the dining room table as a family is good for our children's development, or that growing our own radishes creates a more nutritious radish. We can feel it. Life becomes so loud with demands that the quiet things, the inherently good things that take more time and effort (and all for the better), get pushed aside as inconsequential. We have to follow our intuition to get out of that noise and back to a place where we connect to that which we can't live without. We are indelibly tied to the land, and we still rely on it for survival. We may as well get to know it, savor it, cultivate it gently and deferentially, and above all: Enjoy it.

As you use this book to dictate your own gardening path and preferences, keep in mind that there is always much to learn. You will never be done with wondering and trying, but now you have a field guide to help you breathe life into an idea and give a cadence to your scattered notions. To start, start small. To fail, fail fast. Try everything, and know you'll forget half of what you just read, so thumb back through at the start of each season, check your dog-eared pages, and finally, don't forget to make the chive salt.

Acknowledgments

I am deeply humbled by the generosity of those who have taken me under their wing and taken a chance on me. But first, thank *you* for reading this book. I hope it brings blessings to you in many forms—truly, you matter. Huge gratitude for my husband, Joe, for his patience in this process, for listening to me talk about it for months, and for letting me be me. You make me better and you love me in a way I didn't ever dream was possible. Thank you to my three children for cheering me on and inspiring me endlessly. You've made me brave, and you each uniquely impact our world—it is my greatest honor to bear witness to that.

Thank you so much to Rachel Weber and Ryan McEnaney for leading me to Jessica Walliser, my editor. Jessica, thank you for seeing my potential, expanding me into knowing that I could do this, and for letting Baby Duke join us in many meetings. Thank you so much to Kami Arant for being a source of unbridled enthusiasm and encouragement—also, for taking so many photos over the years! You make it all look so beautiful— an equal match only for the beauty of your pure spirit.

Behind the scenes, working inside my mind, is the ever-present thought that if I can dream it up, I can do it. Mom, you placed that there and I am so grateful to you for not only that but also for the endless support and faith in me. "Lue unco." Den, you've always loved me most and carried so much excitement for all my interests. You are such a gift. Thank you to my Dad, RayLynne, and Aunt Carol for carrying an invisible light for me. I feel your presence in my life daily.

A big thank-you to my mentors and overall supportive characters who let me call them and unwind all the ideas and doubts and nonsense, as well as talk gardening and life: Alyssa Jones, Natalie Kovarik, Annette Thurmon, Jill Ragan, Pamela Martinelli, Kristina and Jen Kittle, and Elizabeth Hays. So much love for my St. Ed's mamas—you cheered for me and my children through all of this, celebrating each milestone. Your friendships have changed me forever and I can't believe I got to do some life with you all.

And finally, what got me here. I have the utmost gratitude for my Kitchen Garden Society members and social media community. Your support for me is something I never want to take for granted, and without you, I may never have had the chance to live so fully into my purpose. That you allow me to speak into your lives, or simply be a fifteen-second presence in your day, is not held lightly. Of all the people to invest in, I am deeply grateful you have taken a chance on me, shared your love for gardening, and kept some space in your heart for the magic of it all.

About the Author

Bailey Van Tassel (@baileyvantassel) is founder of The Kitchen Garden Society and host of The Garden Culture podcast. She shares her gardening skills online, as well as her personal story of growing up on a farm and yet ending up reluctantly in suburbia. Determined to bloom where she is planted, Bailey focuses on kitchen gardening and cut flowers, showcasing how you can grow in any amount of space with a limited amount of time. She gardens with her three young children beside her, believing that living seasonally and staying grounded to the natural world is vitally important to creating a meaningful life no matter where you are.

Index

cucumbers
    borage and, 48, 116
    companion planting, 45
    direct sowing, 71
    as Face plant, 42
    growing temperatures, 25
    harvesting, 85, 131
    light and, 32
    pickling, 155
    plants per person, 43
    prioritizing, 53
    pruning, 82
    school gardens with, 165
    seeds from, 67
curing, 134–135
cut-and-come-again harvesting, 49, 85, 130–131

D

dahlias, 85, 110, 121
daisies, 121
dandelions, 28, 81, 143
decomposed granite (DG), 35
dehydrators, 105
delphiniums, 91
design. *See* planning
dianthus, 91, 116, 121
dibber tool, 87
dill, 45, 163
dino dig activity, 149
direct sowing, 71–72
diseases. *See also* pests
    airflow and, 82
    journaling, 95
    mid-season tending and, 79
    seed catalogs and, 43
    soil and, 133
    variety and, 96
dividing, 88, 91
dogwood, 88
Dried Flower and Herb Pasta recipe, 152
drip irrigation, 33

E

Easy Chicken Stock recipe, 154
echinacea (coneflower), 88, 91, 110, 117
edging details, for in-ground gardening, 32
edible flowers, 109–110, 152
eggplant
    growing temperatures, 25
    harvesting, 131
    as Joker plant, 42
    plants per person, 43
    seasons and, 92
elderflower, 26, 28, 117

F

Face plants, 42, 49
fairy doors, 37, 39, 147

fava beans, 71, 82
fennel, 130, 143, 163
fertilizer. *See also* soil
    comfrey fertilizer, 80, 81, 123
    edible flowers and, 109
    essential nutrients, 63
    selecting, 63
    shadow as, 88
    side-dressing, 80–81
    soil amendments with, 80
    synthetic fertilizers, 109, 122
    wool pellets, 63
fish emulsion, 81
flash freezing, 136
floral ice cubes, 121
Florida weave trellises, 55
flowers. *See also specific types*
    arranging, 111–112
    beneficial insects and, 116
    Calendula and Chamomile Salve, 118–120
    children and, 53, 120
    companion planting, 91
    direct sowing, 71
    dividing, 91
    Dried Flower and Herb Pasta recipe, 152
    edible flowers, 109–110, 152
    floral ice cubes, 121
    flower crown activity, 149
    flower presses, 117
    germination, 109
    gift tag project, 120–121
    light and, 32
    medicinal flowers, 117–118, 118–120
    overhead sprinklers for, 74
    overview of, 143
    pinching, 84
    as Plains plants, 42
    pressing, 117
    seed germination, 109
    symmetry with, 48
    "thrillers, fillers, and spillers," 111
    weaving activity, 148
    wildflower balls, 148
foraging, 26–28
freezing, 136
frost dates, 64, 67, 68, 71

G

garden bundles, 159
garden counting activity, 149
garlic
    Classic Marinara, 154–155
    companion planting, 45, 143
    crop rotation, 50
    curing, 135
    Easy Chicken Stock, 154
    garlic spray, 122–123
    growing temperatures, 25
    growing time, 42

harvesting, 131
one-pot gardens and, 164
plants per person, 43
The Quick Pickle, 155
versatility of, 42
garlic spray, 122–123
geraniums, 85
germination. *See also* seedlings
  dibber tool, 87
  flowers and, 109
  hoop covers and, 80, 92
  indoor starting stations and, 68
  journaling, 95, 96
  multi-sowing and, 70
  radishes, 165
  soil moisture and, 67, 84
  temperature and, 24–25, 64, 67
  timing, 67
  vermiculite and, 84
gift tag project, 120–121
globe artichokes, 110
goals, planning and, 41
gopher wire, 92–93
grapes, 143
grasshoppers, 92
green beans, 131, 136
greenhouses, for seedlings, 72
green onions, 85, 130, 158
greens
  beet greens, 130
  crop priority and, 53
  crop rotation and, 50
  cut-and-come-again harvesting, 85, 130
  garden bundles with, 159
  growing temperatures, 25
  harvesting, 85, 130, 132, 133
  one-pot gardens, 164
  pruning, 82
  seasons and, 19–20
  soil amendments for, 80
grid maps, 33, 44
grow lights, 67, 68
grubs, 93

H

hand forks, 87
hand-watering, 33, 73, 74
hardening off, 67, 68
hardiness zones, 39
harvesting
  bulbs, 131
  children and, 120, 131
  cut-and-come-again harvesting, 49, 130–131
  flavor and, 132
  flowers, 133
  frequency of, 84
  fruits, 131
  greens, 132, 133
  head vegetables, 131

herbs, 85, 128, 130, 155
  interplanting, 49, 50
  overview, 85
  ripeness and, 132
  ripping out, 133
  root vegetables, 130, 132, 133
  seed vegetables, 131
  stem vegetables, 130
  succession planting, 49, 50
  time of day and, 132–133
  timing of, 132–133
  tools for, 86
  tubers, 130–131
healing baskets, 118
heat mats, 67, 68
hedge trimmers, 86
herbal steams, 106–107
herbs. *See also specific types*
  "crunchiness" and, 122
  cut-and-come-again harvesting, 85, 130
  Dried Flower and Herb Pasta, 152
  drying method, 105
  garden bundles and, 159
  harvesting, 85, 128, 130, 155
  herbed breads, 139
  Herbed Salts, 151
  interplanting, 91
  as Plains plants, 42, 49
  prioritizing, 53
  seed organization, 95
  simmer pots with, 22
  snippers for, 86
  steams, 106–107, 123
  tea herbs, 102
  tiny herb gardens, 163, 165
  twine for, 87
holly, 111
homeowners associations (HOAs), 157
honeysuckle, 111
hoops, 67, 72, 80, 87, 92
hornworms, 92, 93
hostas, 91

I

ice scoopers, 87
in-ground gardens
  bed design, 36
  benefits of, 33
  edging details, 32
  no-dig method, 62
  number plates, 37
  pathways for, 32, 33, 35
  planning, 32, 33, 35
  space measurements, 32
  till-once method, 62
interplanting, 49, 50, 80, 81, 91
irises, 91
irrigation
  automatic irrigation, 73–74